# the tickle fingers

# Kids' Cookbook

# the tickle fingers

# Kids' Cookbook

## Hands-on Fun in the Kitchen for **4-7**s

### Annabel Woolmer

**V**ermilion
LONDON

To my two little chefs. You asked me for a book you could cook from yourselves. Here it is, with all my love xx

10 9 8 7 6 5 4 3 2 1

Vermilion, an imprint of Ebury Publishing,
20 Vauxhall Bridge Road,
London SW1V 2SA

Vermilion is part of the Penguin Random House group of companies whose addresses can be found at global. penguinrandomhouse.com

Penguin
Random House
UK

First published by Vermilion in 2019

www.penguin.co.uk

A CIP catalogue record for this book is available from the British Library

ISBN 9781785042355

Colour origination by BORN Ltd
Printed and bound in China by C & C Offset Printing Co., Ltd

Penguin Random House is committed to a sustainable future for our business, our readers and our planet. This book is made from Forest Stewardship Council® certified paper.

Produced by Bookworx
Project editor: Susan McKeever
Project designer: Peggy Sadler

Misc photography credits: Caroline Freebairn, Alex Ginn, Charlie Slight, Simon Gilbert, Kat Gilbert, Jo Spry, Clare Catto, Kate Hillson and Bex Carter

# Contents

# Introduction: why cook with young children?

'Is their diet good enough?' This question pops into my head almost every time I think about what I'm feeding my children.

--------------------------------------------------------------

It's drummed into us as parents: they must have five-a-day, no, actually seven-a-day (who knows how many recommended portions of fruit and veg it will be by the time you're reading this). Diabetes, obesity and tooth decay are on the rise. Even if it's not said, I hear the implication: the parents are to blame – why aren't they feeding their children properly?

There are lots of complicated and interrelated reasons for poor diet in children such as food industry marketing, the convenience and cheapness of processed food, poor education and skills – I will leave others better qualified to go into it all. I come at this as a parent of two young children who knows what they should be eating, is comfortable resisting pester power, knows how to cook healthily on a budget, and yet still needs all the help I can get when it comes to getting them to eat a varied and balanced diet, particularly vegetables and fish.

Part of the problem is that healthy eating has been made into such a big deal. In raising public awareness – which must be a good thing – we and our children are being bombarded with the message that healthy foods like fruit and veg are 'special' foods, something different from everything else we eat, and a source of worry if we don't eat enough. The trouble with this is that people, especially children, are natural rebels. Anything you're told isn't good for you, probably makes

'Part of the problem is healthy eating has been made into such a big deal.'

you think: 'This is something I am going to like.' Anything you're told you must have because it's good for you is something to tolerate, but not necessarily look forward to or enjoy.

This message is reinforced over and over again. Take the children out for a meal and nine times out of ten their 'kids' meal' won't come with vegetables. Or if it does, it will be baked beans or possibly a few cucumber or carrot sticks if you're lucky. The message here is that this is a treat so vegetables wouldn't be part of that because vegetables aren't a treat. How many of us, myself included, have resorted to 'finish your ... and then you can have something sweet'? Again, the message is that healthy foods are something to endure to reach what you really want. For those rigid non-vegetable eaters, there are endless recipes for 'hidden vegetable' dishes. In other words, the way for children to eat vegetables is to trick them into thinking they're not eating them. While it's great that they're eating veg, unfortunately they don't know they are so they still see vegetables as something to tolerate or avoid.

I frequently hear parents in cooking workshops say things like, 'I hate touching fish' or 'I'm scared of cooking chicken.' It makes me wonder whether a reason for opting for processed or ready-made food, apart from the convenience, is this dislike or lack of confidence in handling raw ingredients. The problem for children is, if their primary exposure to foods like meat and fish are in sausage casing or wrapped in breadcrumbs, they too can grow up with the same anxieties, which largely come from lack of familiarity.

So what is the solution? How do we get children to eat more of, and even learn to love, the things that are good for them? I don't have a silver bullet. I wish I had. All I know is there are things we can do that help and things that don't. The number one way I've found to encourage

a more positive relationship with all food, and especially fruit and vegetables, is getting children hands-on and having fun with food on their own terms through cooking.

I wrote my first book, *The Tickle Fingers Toddler Cookbook*, because I wanted my children's early food years to be about exploring and enjoying everyday food. I wanted to expose them to as many new flavours and dishes as possible. I wanted to make them feel involved and engaged with the food they were eating to encourage them to feel excited and intrigued about trying things. I did this by creating recipes that were simple and fun so they could enjoy getting hands-on and familiar with all kinds of ingredients from a very young age. Getting them cooking young has definitely paid off. They don't like everything (who does?), but are generally happy to taste anything and are used to eating a variety of things. They are interested in food, and now aged six and eight enjoy creating their own recipes.

*'I wanted to make them feel involved and engaged with the food they were eating.'*

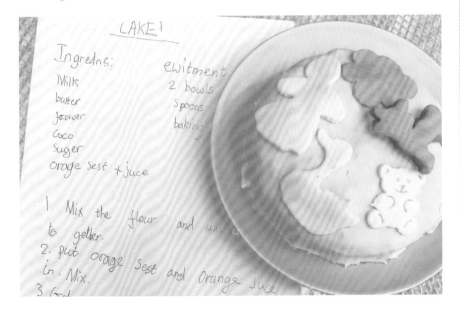

## TIPS FOR GETTING CHILDREN TO LOVE FOOD

### 1 Don't stress!
Don't make food that you want children to eat, like vegetables, into a battleground. Make them a 'no big deal' part of everyday eating. Children pick up on the smallest of signals. If they sense that you see a particular food as different and something you really want them to have, they will treat it differently too.

### 2 Get to know different foods
Children like familiarity. If something looks weird or they don't know what it is, they are biologically programmed to be suspicious about it. Cooking with a new food is the best way to get hands-on and familiar with what something looks, smells and feels like, making it more likely that they'll give it a taste.

### 3 Have fun with food
Don't underestimate the impact emotions can have. Pressure, frustration, impatience, or even cajoling can be counter-productive. Instead, create positive associations by getting children to have fun with food through activities like gardening, shopping and cooking.

### 4 Let them choose
Children aren't going to love everything. Does it matter that they love broccoli, but are not so keen on sprouts? As long as they are eating a range of vegetables, where possible, let them have some choice about what they want to put in a dish. It makes them feel like the dish is 'theirs', increasing the chances of them engaging positively with the end result.

If one of the solutions to broadening children's diet is for them to cook things themselves, the problem is finding everyday, easy recipes for them to follow. To get the full benefit from cooking, children need to be as involved as possible. If a recipe is too complicated or needs too much adult intervention, it can defeat the point. Finding a cake or biscuit recipe that is doable by a five or six year old is fairly easy. But finding a broad range of recipes for younger children to cook is more difficult. With that in mind, this book is a selection of family favourites that my children love to cook and eat, designed and written to be done by children aged around four and over.

I am a great believer in the 'everything in moderation' adage and in the importance of children developing a love of all food. So while all the recipes involve getting up close and hands-on with lots of different ingredients (particularly fruit, veg, fish and meat), not all the recipes are 'healthy' and there are a few once-in-a-while treats.

Some of the dishes may include things some children aren't used to eating. This is intentional. I haven't sought to trick them into eating new things by disguising ingredients or making them look like more familiar dishes. I want them to learn to love the rich diversity of ingredients and flavours there are in the world. I have also tried to include dishes that are not only fun to make, but also easily adapted so they can have fun experimenting and creating their own versions. It is only when children are happy to explore and try anything that they can grow a true love of real food and ingredients. And this for me is my parenting goal, not how many bites of broccoli I managed to persuade them to eat today.

*Annabel*

> 'To get the full benefit from cooking, children need to be as involved as possible.'

# All you need to know

Before you get started, particularly if this is the first time you've cooked with young children, have a look at the next few pages where I will give some handy tips and info on getting the most out of this book.

## NOTE TO THE LITTLE CHEFS

This book has lots of easy, yummy recipes to try, but can you make them even better? Follow the recipe, try it and then come up your own ideas. Perhaps you'd like to ...

• make it with a different fruit or vegetable?

• add something else in?

• form it into a different shape?

• serve it with a different thing?

• decorate it in a different way?

Ask your adult cooking helper to let us know what ideas you come up with and what worked and what didn't! @cookwithtots

# How to cook with children

Many people worry about cooking with children, perhaps because of a lack of time or patience, fear that it will be stressful or memories of past bad experiences.

Here are a few tips based on my own experiences that should help to avoid any stress and make cooking with young children an easy, fun and positive part of family life.

### Make them the head chef

There's a critical difference between cooking with children and children helping in the kitchen. I've come across lots of 'cooking with children' articles that simply list what kitchen jobs children can do at what age. Helping out around the house is an important part of growing up and there are huge benefits to being in the kitchen picking up cooking skills – it's how I learnt to cook. However, if their only involvement in cooking is doing the odd task, children risk seeing cooking as a chore, rather than a fun thing to do. Try switching the roles. Rather than them being your sous chef, make them the head chef and yourself their assistant. If they feel in charge and in control of what they are making, they are much more likely to engage with and enjoy what they're doing.

### Keep it simple

You can't make them the head chef if what they're making is so hard or unsafe you need to jump in all the time. There's nothing more demoralising for a young cook than trying to make something then feeling like they've failed because they have to keep asking an adult to

*'You can't make them the head chef if what they're making is so hard or unsafe you need to jump in all the time.'*

do it for them. Choose short recipes where children can do each step with no or minimal help. The recipes in this book, for example, avoid sharp knives and largely avoid cooking at the hob (except for a few recipes for older children to start learning this). Keeping things simple also means thinking about how the recipe is presented. Cookbooks, even children's cookbooks, often come with confusing layouts or technical language. This book tries to use simple language so that children can start to follow what they need to do themselves.

## Give them choices

This is where you need to think about the endgame. Is it: 'I want my child to be able to follow a recipe'? Or is it: 'I want my child to develop a knowledge and love of food to set them up for their adult lives'? For me it's the latter, because it gives them the confidence to do their own

thing. Children love being creative and it really helps them engage with what they're doing. This doesn't mean allowing them to dictate what they cook. If I did that, all my eldest would cook is multiple varieties of chocolate cake. It means giving them the confidence and knowledge to make choices and adjustments to a dish. You could select an ingredient and ask them to choose something to cook with it. You could pick a dish and ask them to choose appropriate ingredients to go in it. Or you could find an occasion and get them to choose the menu. If you're feeling brave, get them to create their own recipe from scratch and let them make it. I often allow my children to choose what we're eating, even if I'm making it. They love poring over cookbooks and writing out menus and shopping lists. Lots of the recipes in this book work with a range of different ingredients to make it easier for them to get creative.

*'Try to strike a balance between giving tips and suggestions and allowing them to do it their way.'*

## Let go

I know it's easy to say 'let them be the head chef', but it's hard in practice. It takes longer and there's usually more mess (although I'm actually a messier cook than my eight year old). But if you've kept things simple, it won't take that much longer and mess can be contained and cleared up. Set everything up so that your little chefs keep to one place, and remember that you'd have to wipe down the kitchen anyway, no matter who was cooking. Encourage them to be careful and organised, but unless they're going crazy, try to resist getting stressed at mess; it's far better that they're relaxed and enjoying themselves.

Children might do something less than perfectly, or you might know a different or better way to do something. Try to strike a balance between giving tips and suggestions and allowing them to do it their way. Ask yourself: does it matter? Is what they're doing safe? Are they getting the job done? Will it make the recipe fail? If all those things are covered, then leave them to it.

## Focus on taste, not looks

Try to encourage your child to focus on the way a dish tastes, rather than how it looks. The worlds of Pinterest and Instagram have put a lot of emphasis on a dish looking beautiful and appetising. The problem with picking food to cook on looks alone is that you miss out some delicious, simple dishes that perhaps look a bit 'boring'. And more importantly, without a food stylist arranging every little detail, the dish almost certainly won't come out looking like it did in the book or online. When this happens, you run the risk of children feeling like they've failed, even if the food tastes delicious.

There's a balance to be struck because of the link between our eyes and our taste buds – children are unlikely to want to cook something that looks awful. However, to avoid disappointment, I've tried to show the dishes in the photos as they actually are, and roughly how they're likely to come out for them.

## Engage them beyond the dish

Instilling an interest in food is about more than just cooking. Cooking is a platform for learning about and appreciating the world around us. Children love to understand the wider context: perhaps there's a story behind the dish they're making? It might come from a different country or region. Is there a bit of history or a legend attached? Do they know where the main ingredients come from? Is it something they could grow themselves, or does it come from another part of the world? If so, where and how does it get to us? Is the ingredient grown or does it come from an animal? Has it been processed in some way – what's happened to it? What do they know about the different types of food and what each one gives to their body? When they're putting their own ideas into a dish, can they use their basic nutrition knowledge to make sure they balance the meal? Do they know what an ingredient is going

*'Try to encourage your child to focus on how a dish tastes, rather than how it looks.'*

to taste like – sweet, sour, salty, etc.? Can they talk about taste and combining flavours?

The options for engagement are huge. See page 118 for some foodie activity ideas and resources.

*'Always read the recipe through first yourself to make sure you are happy with everything they have to do.'*

### A job for each child

I have two children who both love to cook. If one is doing it, the other one usually wants to join in. Sometimes they want to work as a team and that's great. But often they end up bickering and I end up stressed and frustrated. Practising teamwork is an important learning point. However, with cooking, I sympathise with them not wanting to share because they are creating something. I wouldn't usually expect them to work together on the same drawing or painting – I'd give them two bits of paper so they can express themselves and feel that sense of pride in what they've created. The same goes for cooking a dish, especially when there is scope for them to select ingredients or decide on decoration. So where possible, I try to negotiate them cooking separately – for instance, one could make a main dish and the other a pudding. Or you could split the ingredients in half.

## Safety in the kitchen

I've talked a lot about giving children control – making them the head chef – and my approach to cooking is to give them the confidence to do their own thing. However, this is only possible if they understand and respect certain rules that keep them safe. You may want to create your own, but below are my top six suggestions:

### TOP SIX SAFETY RULES FOR LITTLE CHEFS

1 Always make sure a grown-up is close by and knows what you're doing.

2 Do not use anything sharp like a knife, peeler or grater until you have learnt to use it safely and a grown-up has said it's okay. (Note: you can chop many things with a table knife or child-safe scissors instead.)

3 Always ask a grown-up to help you put things in and out of the oven and microwave and to help you while cooking on the hob.

4 Always keep raw meat away from other ingredients and wash your hands and the surfaces after touching it.

5 Taste and try as you cook, but do not taste or lick raw meat or anything that has been in contact with it.

6 Do not put your hands inside tins – the inside of the rim is very sharp. Use a spoon to scrape out the contents or ask a grown-up to do it for you. Do not put your hands inside a food processor when the blade is in place.

While I have written the recipes with a young age range in mind and split them into difficulty levels, every child is different. You are best placed to decide what they are capable of doing safely. Always read the recipe through first yourself to make sure you are happy with everything they have to do. The idea is to cook together. You might be relegated to sous chef to their head chef, but they should never be left unsupervised.

### Where to cook

Think about where the children are going to cook. Kitchen worktops are high and if they're anything like mine, are full of things to fiddle with and get distracted by, some of which are potentially dangerous. Make your life easier by either clearing a space on the worktop or getting them to work at a table. Then only provide them with what they need to make that dish. The 'Adult Prep' section in each recipe tells you what they will need. The other advantage of defining a clear space is that they're more likely to stick to one place, thereby containing mess.

## What you need

You don't need lots of specialised equipment to cook with children, but there are a few things that do make things easier.

### USEFUL EQUIPMENT

1 **Silicone cupcake cases.** You can use these for so many things (e.g. cakes, jellies, yoghurt pots or biscuit moulds) and they are much easier than paper ones, which tend to stick to the spoon when you try to fill them.

2 **Measuring cups and spoons.** Using American-style cups and spoons to measure out things like liquids and dry ingredients is quicker and easier than scales. All children have to do is fill the right cup to level the right number of times. See page 116 for more information on this.

3 **Child-safe knives.** Children can use a normal table knife for all the recipes in this book to allow them to practise knife skills in relative safety, but be aware that even a blunt table knife can hurt. However, not using a sharp knife limits how much they can do. It is difficult to give an age when children can start using sharp knives because it depends mostly on their dexterity and maturity. Child-safe knives are a useful middle ground until they are ready for sharp knives. You can buy them online and in kitchenware shops. They have serrated edges that would still cut a finger that got in the way, but are less likely to cause a significant wound. They cut more easily than blunt table knives and are a good way to teach them to respect knives.

4 **Silicone baking mat.** These are well worth the investment. I have yet to find a lining paper for baking trays that works as well. When a child has invested time and emotion into making a masterpiece, it's upsetting and demoralising if it then sticks to the tray or tin and gets damaged.

5 **Flour dredger.** It's messy putting hands in a bag of flour if you only need a bit for sprinkling. Having the flour ready in a dredger makes it much easier for children to sprinkle flour on a surface or rolling pin to prevent sticking.

6 **Handled grater.** These are much better than box graters for children as they lower the risk of grated fingers. You can also buy handled peelers/choppers for apples and potatoes and others for finely chopping herbs.

# Cooking task tips

It can be hard to explain how to do basic cooking tasks we take for granted, such as breaking eggs. Refer to these tips when teaching children how to do a particular task.

---

### Breaking eggs – pull apart, don't crush

To avoid lots of shell in the mix, tell children to pull the egg apart, rather than smash it open. Get them to knock the egg on the side of the bowl, put their thumbs in the crack and then pull the egg open, like they're knocking on a door and then opening it. Make sure they open the egg over the bowl. If you're worried about egg going everywhere put a large plate underneath to catch any spills. It's then an easy job to tip the spilt egg back into the bowl.

### Brushing – think painting

The main reasons for needing to brush are spreading oil onto a pan to grease it or glazing something like pastry or bread with milk or whisked egg. The key thing to learn is to brush evenly and sparingly. Get children to think of it like painting, where they would scrape excess paint off the brush before painting and would cover a whole area.

### Chopping – get those fingers out of the way!

All the chopping in this book can be done with a table knife or child-safe knife (see page 21 for more on these), but even these can hurt if children are not careful. In any case, it's important they practise safe knife skills to prepare them for using sharp knives later. The main things they need to learn when chopping are holding the food while

tucking all their fingers out of the way (making the hand look like a claw) and always chopping down onto the chopping board. Get them into the habit of every time they go to chop thinking, 'If I chop now, where will the knife go?' If it's in a finger, arm or into the air, then they need to adjust and think again. Often they start carefully and then get distracted. Don't expect them to chop for too long and encourage them to keep talking out loud about where their fingers are and where the knife is going to ensure they stay focused.

The downside of table and child-safe knives is their bluntness. You will need to teach children to do more of a sawing action and apply more downward pressure than when chopping with sharp knives.

### Combining butter and sugar – soft butter is the key

This is the first step to making many cakes and biscuits and therefore a key baking skill. You can do this in a food processor or with an electric whisk, but the hands-on way works well if you bear a few things in mind. First, make sure the butter is soft but not melted, as melting changes the way the butter works. Take it out of the fridge at least an hour before cooking, or soften it in the microwave using its lowest power. Second, get children to use a wooden rather than silicone spoon as the hardness of a wooden spoon makes it easier to work the butter. Rather than simply mixing, get them to do a squish and stir action – squish the butter with the back of the spoon, then mix. The key is to get the butter and sugar completely mixed together, and preferably looking a bit fluffy.

### Cookie cutting – line them up

My children always seem to cut out a shape in the middle of the dough first, have no space to cut out any more and then have to roll out again. The problem with this is the more they work pastry or biscuit dough,

*'Rather than simply mixing, get them to do a squish and stir action – squish the butter with the back of the spoon, then mix.'*

the more chewy it becomes. If you can, get them to mark out where they're going to cut first by very lightly pressing the cutter on the dough. Challenge them to see how many they can fit in one go. Or you could do the marking out for them and then get them to match the cutter with the outlines. Having said that, it isn't the end of the world if they end up rolling out multiple times. If it's making them happy to do their own thing, go with it.

### Decorating – let them loose!

This is usually where children can be most creative and where I have to force myself to let go of my inner control freak. Lay out a few bits and bobs for them to use and let them get on with it. You might think their cakes or biscuits look like a disaster zone, but they'll be proud and happy with their creations.

### Dividing – make it a circle

Children will sometimes need to divide something up, e.g. bread dough or cutting a cake into slices. If it isn't already, tell them to form what they're portioning into a circle. Then get them to cut the circle in half for two portions, quarters for four portions, eighths for eight portions. A circle usually makes it easier for them to visualise.

### Dusting – make it snow

This is the process of scattering a small amount of dry ingredients like flour to stop dough sticking to the worktop or rolling pin, or sprinkling icing sugar on a cake to decorate. The difficulty is getting children to use a small amount and getting it evenly dusted. The best way I've found is to use a shaker or dredger. They're cheap to buy and mean all they have to do is shake the dredger over the area they want to dust. The dredger stops everything coming out in one go and is fun because it looks like they're making it 'snow'. If you don't have a dredger, then simply use

*'If you can, get them to mark out where they're going to cut first by very lightly pressing the cutter on the dough.'*

a sieve and get children to gently tap the side to get the flour or icing sugar to dust. Be prepared for a bit of flour or sugar to go elsewhere though if they're using this method!

### Flavour selection – check before tasting

There are some recipes in this book which ask children to decide on their own flavours. When thinking and choosing ingredients, encourage them to use their senses: smell, look, touch and if safe, taste. If they're reluctant tasters, get them to place the options on the tip of their tongue. Tasting ingredients and exploring flavour is an important part of cooking but bear in mind that there are some foods that can cause a sore tummy or even food poisoning if eaten raw, e.g. potatoes, eggs, flour, kidney beans and especially meat. Make them aware that it isn't always okay to taste. Teach them the big no-no, which is raw meat, and then get them into the habit of checking before they taste something. If in doubt about whether something is safe, look it up or say no.

### Folding – mix it gently

This is a cooking term that is used a lot. It basically means mixing gently. It's important when, for example, they've whisked something to make it fluffy and then need to mix in another ingredient without knocking out all the air they've just whisked in. Rather than thinking 'round and round' for mixing, get children to think 'up and over' – i.e. lifting the mix from the bottom and putting it on top. Always fold slowly and for a short time – stop as soon as the ingredient is mixed in.

### Forming and shaping – squish, squash and squeeze

Your young chefs need to get their hands in the mix and squish. It is the opposite of 'tickling' where they need to use finger tips only – here they'll need the whole hand and especially the palms. Get them to take as big a handful as possible and squish and squeeze until the dough,

pastry or burger comes together. They are at a disadvantage with smaller hands. If there's a large amount of mix to bring together, it might be a good idea for them to do half and then the other half.

### Handling raw fish – keep it positive

Lots of people dislike handling raw fish, primarily because of the texture and getting smelly hands. If you have a problem with it, try not to let that show when cooking with children. Most children will find the texture of raw fish interesting and it won't necessarily occur to them that it could be unpleasant unless they see an adult react. That said, there are some children who have a genuine fear of getting certain things on their hands. Cooking can be a good way to encourage them to touch new things, but never push it and get them to use spoons or tongs if they really don't want to touch something. As for smelly hands, wash hands with cold water after handling raw fish. Warm water 'cooks' the smell onto hands and makes it linger for longer.

*'Teach them the big no-no, which is raw meat, and then get them into the habit of checking before they taste something.'*

### Handling raw meat – follow the rules and then don't worry

It's easy to worry about handling raw meat, especially poultry, because of the dangers of spreading harmful bacteria. Unless cooking with very young children who like to stuff everything in their mouths, don't let this put you off letting them cook with meat. Just teach them the rules and make sure you supervise more closely. The rules are:

1 Don't wash meat (that just spreads bacteria even further).
2 Don't let other ingredients touch raw meat or where it has been. In other words, after prepping raw meat, clean down the area, or better still keep the raw meat on a designated, separate chopping board that can be removed.
3 Wash hands after touching raw meat and definitely don't lick fingers until they've been washed.

'If they're struggling with stickiness, dust some flour on their hands and the worktop.'

### Juicing – push, twist and turn

If only a little juice is needed from something like an orange, lemon or lime, the easiest thing is to cut it in half or into quarters and then get children to give it a squeeze between their fingers over the bowl. If they need to remove all the juice, then they'll need to use a juicer. I find the best ones are the silicone ones that suction onto the table. Otherwise, they need the dexterity to hold the juicer with one hand and then push, twist and turn the fruit on top with the other. Children often give it a couple of turns and announce it's done. Encourage them to keep going by challenging them to see just how much juice they can get out.

### Kneading – squish, squash and keep going!

Done right, this is a really fun activity for children. Done wrong and they quickly end up in a pickle with dough stuck to everything. They need to do a squishing and squashing action into the worktop or table using only the heel of their hands and never their fingers – dough squished between fingers is tough to remove! The quicker and harder they knead, the less sticky the dough becomes. So if it does go sticky, don't try to remove their stuck hands, just get them to keep going. Often the dough will come loose from their hands of its own accord. If they're struggling with stickiness, dust some flour on their hands and the worktop.

### Measuring – fill it level

Sometimes children will have to use scales to weigh out an ingredient but for the most part, the easiest way to measure is with cups and spoons. They need to identify the right cup or spoon, fill it and then run a hand over the top to make sure it is filled level. Show them the difference between tablespoon (tbsp) and teaspoon (tsp) sizes as they're easy to mix up. For smaller cup measurements, they can just scoop up the ingredient in the appropriate cup, but if using a larger cup, it's easier to put it on the table and fill it up with a spoon.

For liquids, I've tried to keep to cup measurements so children just have to fill them to the top. If they're using a measuring jug, put a bit of tape where they need to fill up to, so it's easier for them to see.

## Mixing – round and round

I think we all assume children are naturals at mixing. Some definitely are but a surprising number aren't and tend to just prod the mix a few times. Get them thinking about going round and round the bowl, perhaps pretending they're driving round a race track, drawing a figure of eight or just making swirls; anything to encourage them to keep going. Make sure they know why they are mixing. For example, if they're mixing in flour, they need to keep going until all the flour disappears. Or if they're just mixing to jumble everything up, then they can stop when they think this has happened.

## Peeling (garlic, root veg) – getting the skin off

Garlic: the easiest way for a child to peel a clove of garlic is to bash it first with a rolling pin or in a pestle and mortar until the skin loosens. Then the skin will almost fall off.

**Root vegetables (using a peeler):** peeling veg with a peeler is a fun job for children who are old enough to respect that it's sharp and know to keep it away from fingers. Use a double-sided peeler so they simply have to lay it on the veg and scrape.

### Rolling – it takes practice

Children often grip the rolling pin so their fingers are in the way when they roll. Encourage them to spread their fingers into 'stars' or a 'butterfly'. Although children's baking sets often come with rolling pins, adult rolling pins are better because they have the room to spread their hands out, and the weight helps them compress the dough as they roll. Children sometimes press too hard when they roll. Don't be surprised if takes them a while to get the hang of rolling out – it takes practice.

### Snipping – keep those fingers out of the way!

It is often easier to snip something than to chop it with a knife and using scissors is great for developing a child's dexterity. It also means you don't need to worry about a chopping board. You can use child-safe scissors to snip up herbs in a cup and also to cut up beans, tomatoes, cooked meats, mushrooms, spring onions or really anything that is soft enough. Most children learn how to use scissors in preschool or school. The usual rules apply with cooking like keeping fingers out of the way and pointing the scissors away from the body.

### Spooning and scraping – how to move sticky mixtures

Moving sticky mixtures from one place to another is best done with two spoons or a spoon and spatula. They need to scoop up the mixture with one spoon and scrape it off into where it is going with the other spoon or spatula. If they're new to cooking, you might want to help by doing either the spooning or the scraping. This is a great skill to get the hang of as they'll need it often in cooking, especially baking.

## Spreading – scrape and spread

Spreading is a useful skill that children can do almost daily, e.g. spreading butter or jam on their own toast in the morning or making their own sandwiches. Sometimes it is easier to explain spreading in terms of 'scraping'.

## Sprinkling – make your hand into a duck's beak

This is the technique for scattering grated cheese on something or decorating with things like icing sprinkles. Get children to hold their hand (formed into a duck beak shape) over the dish or biscuit and rub their thumb over their fingers to sprinkle. The higher they hold their hand, the more spaced out the sprinkle will be.

## Tearing – pull, pull, pull

All children have to think about with tearing is pulling something apart.

## Threading on skewers – keep the point down

The issue with children putting things on skewers is the potential for accidentally skewering their hand. To avoid this get them to spike the ingredient on a chopping board, then keeping the point on the board with one hand, pull the ingredient up the skewer with the other.

## 'Tickle fingers' technique – use a light touch!

To turn flour and butter into the breadcrumb-like texture needed for pastry or crumble, tell the children to rub the flour into the butter with their fingertips. If they squish too hard, they could end up with a lump of dough instead. Tell them to pretend they are 'tickling' the butter into the flour – a process we call 'tickle fingers'. They also use this for crumbling stock cubes.

*'Moving sticky mixtures from one place to another is best done with two spoons or a spoon and spatula.'*

### Using a food processor – mind those blades!

Being able to use a food processor opens up lots of dishes that involve puréeing, blending or finely chopping. They come with safety features, but the sharp blades mean that children still need close supervision, particularly when putting things in and out of the processor bowl. I get them to fill it before I put the blade in and likewise I then remove the blade at the end before they scrape the contents out.

### Using a hob – are they ready yet?

The potential risks for young cooks escalate significantly when using a hob, e.g. burning themselves on the pan, knocking boiling food off the hob or setting their clothing on fire. This is why most of the recipes I like to do with young children avoid them being anywhere near it. However, learning to use a hob safely is an essential part of learning to cook. Cooking at a hob is less about skill and more about maturity and mood. The danger comes when a child gets distracted, has a strop, or doesn't take safety instructions seriously. I know some four year olds who, in the right mood, are easily mature enough. Likewise, I know some ten year olds who wouldn't be safe. Knowing when they're ready or in the right mood is a judgement call.

I wouldn't do a recipe with younger children that involves spending long periods stirring something at the hob. However mature they are, it's hard for them to concentrate for long periods, and lapses of concentration can be dangerous. Likewise, I would avoid recipes that involve very high heat where the food – especially oil –could spit. Start with short, easy recipes that use a low heat like porridge (page 51), soda bread farls (page 81) and quesadillas (page 66) and build up confidence from there. Whatever their confidence level, there should always be an adult with them ready to step in if need be.

'Cooking at a hob is less about skill and more about maturity and mood.'

## Using a microwave – harness their technology skills

Until they are mature and experienced enough to use a hob, a microwave can help younger children cook more things. The risks are fewer than using a hob, but a microwave is still potentially dangerous. They need close supervision, particularly while learning what to do. They need to be aware that the food will remain hot and that they should wait for a minute or so before removing things from the microwave or ask you to do it. They also need to be aware of microwave safety guidelines, such as not putting anything metal inside.

That said, using a microwave is fun for children, and as technical natives, they'll probably soon know more about what the buttons do than you. Apart from learning how to set the timer and start it, a useful thing you can teach them is how to heat things gently in a microwave. This means they can use it to soften butter for baking cakes and to melt chocolate. To do this, they need to learn how to set the microwave to low power (sometimes referred to as 30 per cent power). This will be different from microwave to microwave. If you don't have a microwave, you can use a bain-marie. However, this is really an adult job as it requires hot water on a hob with a bowl balanced on top.

## Whisking – keep going!

You can use a hand-held balloon whisk or an electric whisk. With a hand whisk, children need to tilt the bowl slightly and move the whisk side-to-side in the mixture as quickly as they can. One of the trickier things about whisking is knowing when to stop. For batter, they just need to whisk until there are no lumps and some bubbles forming. For egg whites, they usually need to whisk until they've turned white and look stiff. For egg and sugar, they need to whisk until the mix looks visibly bigger. For cream, they need to whisk until the cream goes from runny to thick enough to form soft peaks. Explain that this takes patience!

*'One of the trickier things about whisking is knowing when to stop.'*

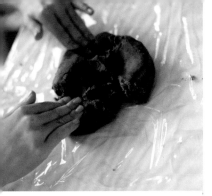

# Adapting recipes for children
This book has recipes that are tailored for children to follow. However, you can also adapt other, more complicated recipes for young children to try.

*'Mushrooms, peppers, green beans, cabbage, broccoli and cauliflower can all be torn.'*

### Language
The fundamentals of most recipes are usually straightforward. However, the biggest stumbling block for children trying to use adult cookbooks is complicated layouts and lengthy or technical language. I get round this by writing out the main points of the recipe in simpler language on a separate bit of paper. It only takes me a couple of minutes and makes such a difference to their sense of independence.

### Separate prep, assembly and cooking
Many recipes involve prepping ingredients, assembling the dish and then cooking it. However, they're not necessarily written that way. To maximise the amount children can do themselves, see if you can re-order the recipe so you prep the ingredients together first (some elements you may have to do and some your child can do). Do the assembly next and allow them to take the lead. And finally, get involved again for the final cooking phase.

### Vegetables
Some vegetables are easy for children to prepare and some are almost impossible without using a sharp knife or par-cooking first. Mushrooms, peppers, green beans, cabbage, broccoli and cauliflower can all be torn. Tomatoes, courgettes and aubergines are just soft enough to chop with

a table knife. Sweetcorn, peas and spinach can be used as they are. However, root vegetables will need to be cooked first before they can be chopped safely. Sometimes, you can make a recipe easier for children to make just by substituting different vegetables.

### Seasoning: what's a pinch?

Getting the seasoning right is tricky for all cooks. Phrases like 'season to taste' or 'add a pinch of salt' don't mean much to young children and an otherwise delicious dish can be ruined by putting too much salt or pepper in. Add the seasoning yourself once the dish is cooked, or try to express the amount of seasoning as a measurement. I have a ⅛ tsp measuring spoon, which, if they don't fill it right to the top, is about a pinch. I usually get them to use this for adding salt and pepper.

## Onions

Onions are the nemesis of cooking with children. They are impossible to chop without a sharp knife, and even then, hard to do well. Plus, they make their eyes water and hurt. But it's difficult to leave them out because they add so much important flavour. You can of course chop the onions for them, or buy them ready chopped. However, there are other ways to add an onion flavour. For a stew or curry, you can use dried onion granules. Or for a fresher onion flavour, you can use spring onions or chives, which can simply be snipped with child-safe scissors.

## Gadgets

I'm not a big fan of using lots of gadgets when cooking with children because I like them to be as hands-on as possible. However, there are some gadgets that will help them to make some recipes that they otherwise couldn't. Mini choppers (manual or electric) are good for finely chopping anything like ginger, carrots, garlic, onion or herbs. Children will need help getting the ingredients in and out, however, because of the sharp blades. Mill graters allow them to grate things like cheese with less chance of grating a finger by mistake. Under supervision, microwaves are useful for heating some things that would otherwise be heated on a hob.

## Size matters

When adapting recipes for children, think about whether you need to cut the quantity down. The recipes in this book, particularly the baking ones, provide smaller quantities than a lot of recipe books. This is intentional. Mixing or whisking larger mixtures takes more effort. Bringing together a large lump of dough with small hands is tricky. Cutting out 20 or 30 biscuits takes time and can become tedious. In other words, how much children are making of something definitely has an impact on difficulty.

*'Bringing together a large lump of dough with small hands is tricky.'*

# How to use this book

I have arranged this book to make it as easy as possible to foster independent cooking for your child. Take a look through these notes before you start, to get the most from the recipes.

-------------------------------------------------

The recipes are divided into five main sections:

**Breakfast fun** A few quick recipes to make in the morning and a few to make ahead of time.

**Light bites** Snacks, picnic and lunch ideas.

**Friends for tea** Savoury and sweet baking treats for parties, playdates or just after-school snacks.

**Family supper** Main dishes for all the family to enjoy.

**Sweet endings** Easy, fruity, crowd-pleasing desserts.

**Each recipe is laid out with:**

**Quantities:** The quantities are generally lower than you'd find in most recipe books. This is to make the recipes easier and less time-consuming to make. Most of the meals are about the right amount for a family of two adults and two younger children.

**Timings:** I have given two timings: how long it will take for the child to prep the dish (Activity) and how long it will need to bake or chill before eating (Oven, Chill, etc.). The activity timing will vary depending on the age and experience of the child, but it should give a steer on which are the really short recipes and which will take a bit longer. It's useful to have an idea of time so you have realistic goals of what can be achieved in a particular window you may have set aside for a cooking session.

*'The activity timing will vary depending on the age and experience of the child.'*

## DIFFICULTY LEVELS

Every recipe has a difficulty level denoted by a tab at the top of the page. Different children find different things more difficult than others, so these are just a general guide.

**Easy Peasy:** perfect for those who've done very little or no cooking or if you're looking for a super-simple recipe.

**Budding Cook:** great for those with a bit of experience or ready to tackle tasks which need more instruction, e.g. using a microwave or rolling out dough.

**Confident Chef:** for those who are ready to learn more advanced tasks, e.g. basic cooking at the hob or kneading. However if you are cooking with a younger or less experienced child, don't discount these because with more adult help, they can be done by anyone.

**Adult prep:** this tells you what you need to do to get the activity ready, including what equipment to lay out. Doing these bits first means your child can get on and enjoy being the head chef when making the dish, without them frequently needing you to do or find something.

**Oven temperatures:** I've given oven temperatures in Celsius, Fahrenheit and gas mark. I haven't given a temperature for using a fan oven because the effect of the fan is different in different ovens. In my current fan oven, which is over a decade old, I find I only need to lower the temperature by about 5 degrees to get the same cooking effect as a standard oven. In some efficient, newer fan ovens, you might need to set the temperature up to 20°C lower to have the same effect. Not very helpful I know, but oven temperatures and timings are a guide and I'm afraid the only answer to the fan temperature question is to get to know your oven.

**Main tasks:** This tells you what the main tasks are in the recipes. It will help you know what children will need to do in the recipe and provides a link to more guidance if they need help mastering a task. Flip back to the Cooking Task Tips section for teaching tips.

**Allergies:** I've listed substitution ideas for the main children's allergies: dairy, eggs, gluten and nuts. If cooking with children who have allergies, you may also find the allergy chart on page 121 useful. This helps you identify the recipes they can cook with no problems, those they need to adapt and those they should avoid. However, even if it says a recipe is okay, check it yourself and check all ingredient labels for allergens as different producers may include different ingredients.

**Variations:** Most of the recipes in this book have been chosen because they can be adapted easily to enable children to experiment with ingredients and their own ideas. In some recipes, I've started them off by giving some ideas for different versions under 'Variations'. Where I've used meat or fish, I've also included a vegetarian (v) suggestion.

**Measurements:** These are in metric and where appropriate in American-style cups and spoons, which can be easier and quicker for younger children to use than scales. All measurements in cups and spoons are level measurements, unless the recipes say otherwise. See page 118 for more on measuring with cups and spoons.

## What's at the back?
Turn to the back of the book and you'll find:
• Activity resources and ideas for engaging children about dishes and ingredients beyond cooking.
• A comprehensive index to help you find recipes, ingredients and more.
• Cups and spoons information and a weight conversion chart.
• An allergy chart.

## And finally ...
Let them be in charge, let them have fun, but never leave them unsupervised while cooking.

# Breakfast fun

This selection of easy recipes for breakfast are also great as snacks at any time of day. There are a few quick ones to make in the morning rush, as well as longer ones to make ahead of time.

 **EASY PEASY**

 **BUDDING COOK**

 **CONFIDENT CHEF**

# Pink smoothie

A thick, filling berry smoothie that makes a great addition to breakfast or a yummy snack or dessert at any time of day.

MAKES 2 or 4
ACTIVITY 10 min

## MAIN TASKS
- Using a food processor
- Spooning and scraping

## VARIATION
Swap raspberries for strawberries or mixed summer fruits.

## ALLERGY INFO

| DAIRY | Use dairy-free yoghurt and milk |
|-------|---------------------------------|
| EGG | No egg |
| GLUTEN | No gluten |
| NUT | Check labels |

## What you need
- 1 banana
- 180g (1½ cups) frozen raspberries
- ½ tsp vanilla extract
- 240g (1 cup) Greek-style yoghurt
- 120ml (½ cup) milk

## Adult prep
Lay out: ingredients, food processor, spatula and 2 large or 4 small drinking glasses.

TOP TIP!
Experiment with different fruits to find your own favourite smoothie combination.

## How to make

1 Peel the banana.

2 Break the peeled banana into chunks and put the chunks into the food processor.

3 Put the raspberries, vanilla extract, yoghurt and milk into the food processor.

4 Whizz the mix in the processor until everything is mixed together and it looks smooth.

Ask an adult to **pour and scrape the smoothie into the glasses**.

# Tropical smoothie

This lighter, refreshing smoothie can be enjoyed throughout the day, and especially when the sun is shining.

## What you need
- 300g (2 cups) frozen mixed tropical or exotic fruit
- 1 orange
- 240ml (1 cup) water

## Adult prep
- Cut the orange in half.
- Lay out: ingredients, food processor, juicer, spatula and 2 large or 4 small drinking glasses.

## How to make

**1** Put the frozen fruit into the food processor.

**2** Use a juicer to squeeze the juice from the orange.

**3** Pour the fresh orange juice into the food processor.

**4** Pour the water into the food processor.

**5** Whizz the mix in the processor until everything is mixed together and it looks smooth.

Ask an adult to **pour and scrape the smoothie into the glasses.**

MAKES 2 or 4
ACTIVITY 10 min

## MAIN TASKS
- Juicing
- Using a food processor

## ALLERGY INFO

| DAIRY | No dairy |
|---|---|
| EGG | No egg |
| GLUTEN | No gluten |
| NUT | Check labels |

### TOP TIP!
If you want a thicker smoothie, add less water. If you want a runny smoothie, add more.

# Pick 'n' mix granola

No more picking the bits you don't like out of your granola!
With this one you make it exactly how you want by tasting and
choosing your favourite ingredients.

MAKES 250g
ACTIVITY 15 min
15 min
OVEN

## MAIN TASKS
- Flavour selection
- Measuring
- Chopping
- Mixing

## VARIATION
Add any dried fruit, nuts or seeds
to the list of possible ingredients to
choose from.

## ALLERGY INFO

| DAIRY | No dairy |
|---|---|
| EGG | No egg |
| GLUTEN | Use gluten-free oats |
| NUT | Do not use nuts and check labels |

## What you need
- 100g (1 cup) oats
- 1 tbsp vegetable oil
- 1 tbsp runny honey
- 2 tbsp mixed peel (optional)
- 2 tbsp currants (optional)
- 2 tbsp dried cranberries (optional)
- 2 tbsp raisins or sultanas (optional)
- 2 tbsp mixed chopped nuts (optional)
- 6 dried apricots (optional)
- 6 dried prunes (optional)

## Adult prep
- Preheat oven to 180°C/350°F/Gas 4.
- Lay out: ingredients, mixing bowl, mixing spoon, baking tray, sheet of foil, table knife, chopping board and a pot or jar with lid.

## How to make

**1** Put the oats, oil and honey into the bowl and give it a good mix.

**2** Put the sheet of foil onto the baking tray.

**3** Tip the oats on top of the foil and spread them out.

Ask an adult to put the tray into the oven for 10 to 15 minutes. While the oats are cooking ...

**4** Taste and choose 3 or more of the optional ingredients to put in your granola.

**5** If using apricots or dates, tear or chop them into little bits.

**6** If using raisins or sultanas, tear or chop them in half (2 bits).

**7** When the oats are cooked and cool, tip them back into the mixing bowl.

**8** Put your chosen ingredients into the bowl and give it all a good mix.

**9** Tip the granola into the pot or jar and put on the lid ready for breakfast.

# Egg mug

If you want a cooked breakfast but don't have time in the morning rush, a quick egg mug is the answer.

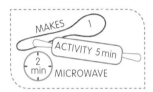

MAKES 1
ACTIVITY 5 min
2 min MICROWAVE

## MAIN TASKS
- Tearing or chopping
- Breaking eggs
- Snipping
- Sprinkling
- Using a microwave

## VARIATION
For an egg mug omelette, add some grated cheese and whisk up the egg mix with a fork before microwaving.

## ALLERGY INFO

| | |
|---|---|
| DAIRY | Use dairy-free spread |
| EGG | Avoid |
| GLUTEN | No gluten |
| NUT | No nut |

## What you need
- ½ tsp butter
- 1 medium mushroom
- 1 egg
- 1 chive

## Adult prep
- Be ready to help with the microwave in Steps 4 and 7.
- Lay out: ingredients, microwave-safe mug or ramekin, sheet of kitchen roll, table or child-safe knife, chopping board, child-safe scissors and fork (optional).

### TOP TIP!
Make a little gap in the middle of the cooked mushrooms and try to break the egg so the yolk sits in the gap.

## How to make

1 Put the butter into the mug.

2 Wipe the mushroom with kitchen roll to remove any dirt.

3 Tear or chop the mushroom into little bits and put them into the mug.

4 Put the mug into the microwave and cook for 1 minute. Leave the mug to cool for another minute before taking it out.

5 Use child-safe scissors to snip the chive into little bits and sprinkle the bits into the mug.

6 Break the egg into the mug.

7 Put the mug back into the microwave and cook for 50 seconds. N.B. It might need a bit longer or shorter depending on the microwave and thickness of the mug.

Ask an adult to take the mug out of the microwave and scoop the cooked egg onto a plate. Enjoy on its own or with toast.

# Tray-bake pancakes

Usually you need to fry pancakes one at a time in a pan, but these Scotch pancakes, or drop scones, can be baked in the oven so they're ready in one go.

## What you need
- 65g (½ cup) self-raising flour
- ½ tbsp sugar
- 60ml (¼ cup) milk
- 1 egg

## Adult prep
- Preheat oven to 220°C/425°F/Gas 7.
- Lay out: ingredients, mixing bowl, whisk, tablespoon, baking tray and silicone baking mat or baking paper.

### TOP TIP!
Work out where to space out the pancakes on the tray before you dollop the mix on because once on, you won't be able to move them until they're cooked.

## How to make

**1** Put the flour, sugar and milk into the bowl.

**2** Break the egg into the bowl.

**3** Whisk it all up until the mix is smooth and bubbly.

**4** Put a baking mat or sheet of baking paper onto the baking tray.

**5** Dollop 9 spoonfuls of mix onto the tray. Make sure you space them out as they will get bigger.

Ask an adult to put the tray into the oven for 4 minutes. Turn the pancakes over and put the tray back into the oven for another 3 minutes. If the pancakes are stuck to the paper, turn the whole sheet over to finish the baking. Once cooked through and cooled slightly, they're easier to peel off the paper.

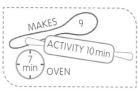

MAKES 9
ACTIVITY 10 min
7 min OVEN

## MAIN TASKS
- Breaking eggs
- Whisking

## TOPPING IDEAS
Butter and jam; avocado mashed with a little bit of lime juice; Greek-style yoghurt, honey and berries.

## ALLERGY INFO

| | |
|---|---|
| DAIRY | Use dairy-free milk |
| EGG | Avoid |
| GLUTEN | Use gluten-free flour |
| NUT | Check labels |

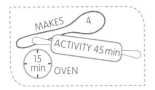

# Basic bread rolls

Home-made bread tastes and smells amazing. Once you've learnt this basic bread roll recipe you can create your own versions. Take a look at 'Variations' for ideas.

**MAKES** 4
**ACTIVITY** 45 min
**15 min** **OVEN**

## MAIN TASKS
- Kneading
- Dividing
- Forming and shaping

## VARIATIONS
For white rolls, use strong white flour (N.B. use 10ml less water). For an Italian flavour, add 1 tsp of olive oil to the dough. To add a topping, brush the dough balls with milk and sprinkle on seeds like poppy or sesame.

## ALLERGY INFO

| DAIRY | No dairy |
| --- | --- |
| EGG | No egg |
| GLUTEN | Avoid |
| NUT | Check labels |

## What you need
- 260g (2 cups) strong wholemeal bread flour
- 1 tsp salt
- 2 tsp instant dried yeast
- 180ml (¾ cup) warm water

## Adult prep
- Preheat oven to 200°C/390°F/Gas 6
- Lay out: ingredients, mixing bowl, mixing spoon, table knife, baking tray and clean tea towel.

### TOP TIP!
You'll probably need to knead the dough for at least 5 minutes, preferably 10, so get those muscles working!

## How to make

1 Put the flour and salt into the bowl and mix.

2 Put the yeast and water into the bowl.

3 Mix it all up into a dough.

4 Tip the dough onto a clean worktop and squish and squash (knead) it until it feels soft and springy, usually for at least 5 minutes. Kneading can be tricky. Find tips on page 28.

5 Cut the dough into quarters (4 bits).

6 Shape each bit into a ball.

7 Put the rolls onto the baking tray and cover with a clean tea towel. Leave them for 30 minutes. This is called 'proving'.

Ask an adult to put the rolls in the oven for 15 minutes or until the bottoms sound hollow when you tap them. Don't worry if they come out denser than shop-bought rolls. Try different spreads on your rolls – butter, jam, peanut butter, cream cheese ...

# Hot choc porridge

This regular breakfast request in our house is an easy and quick recipe to start learning about cooking on the hob. It's delicious with fresh fruit like blueberries, raspberries or strawberries.

## What you need
- 35g (⅓ cup) porridge oats
- 1 tsp hot chocolate powder
- 60ml (⅓ cup) milk
- 60ml (⅓ cup) water
- A handful of fruit

## Adult prep
- Be ready to help children use the hob or do this bit yourself.
- Lay out: ingredients, pan, mixing spoon, bowl, chopping board and table or child-safe knife.

### TOP TIP!

Make this to order because no one likes cold porridge. This recipe is enough for one portion, but you can make lots of portions together, depending on how many want it.

## How to make

1 Put the oats, chocolate powder, milk and water into the pan.

2 Give it all a good mix.

Ask an adult to **help you put the pan onto a low to medium hob and help you cook and serve the porridge.**

3 Heat the porridge until it is gloopy – about 4 or 5 minutes. Mix the porridge a few times while it is cooking to stop it sticking to the bottom. Be careful, do not touch the pan – it will be hot.

4 Carefully spoon and scrape the porridge into the bowl.

5 Chop the fruit into bits. If using strawberries, cut off the green bits and throw them away.

6 Put the chopped fruit and a splash of cold milk onto the cooked porridge to serve.

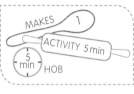

MAKES 1
ACTIVITY 5 min
5 min HOB

## MAIN TASKS
- Mixing
- Using a hob
- Chopping

## ALLERGY INFO

| | |
|---|---|
| DAIRY | Use dairy-free milk and ½ tsp cocoa powder instead of hot chocolate and add a bit of honey to sweeten if required |
| EGG | No egg |
| GLUTEN | Use gluten-free oats |
| NUT | Check labels |

# Light bites

Here are some quick and easy lunch or savoury snack ideas when you're not feeling like a big meal. There are also a few options to make for lunchboxes.

# Cauliflower bhajis

Jazz up cauliflower with a bright yellow covering. These bhajis taste great served with a curry or as a snack or light lunch.

MAKES 12
ACTIVITY 15 min
20 min OVEN

## MAIN TASKS
- Whisking
- Mixing
- Brushing

## ALLERGY INFO

| DAIRY | No dairy |
|-------|----------|
| EGG | No egg |
| GLUTEN | Use gluten-free flour |
| NUT | Check labels, especially garam masala |

## What you need
- 65g (½ cup) self-raising flour
- ⅛ tsp salt
- 1 tsp garam masala
- 1 tsp turmeric
- 120ml (½ cup) water
- 1 small cauliflower, leaves removed
- 1 tsp oil for greasing

## Adult prep
- Preheat oven to 200°C/390°F/Gas 6.
- Lay out: ingredients, mixing bowl, mixing spoon, hand whisk, baking tray and pastry brush.

### TOP TIP!

Turmeric turns everything it touches yellow, including your hands. Make the dish on a mat or board so it doesn't stain the worktop!

## How to make

**1** Put the flour, salt, garam masala and turmeric into the bowl and mix.

**2** Put the water into the bowl and whisk until there are no lumps. This is called 'batter'.

**3** Pull the florets ('trees') off the cauliflower and put them into the bowl. If the florets are large, break or chop them in half.

**4** Mix the florets into the mixture until all of them are covered in batter.

**5** Brush the oil all over the baking tray to grease it.

**6** Put the cauliflower florets onto the baking tray. Make sure they are spaced out.

Ask an adult to **put the tray into the oven and bake for 20 minutes until crispy, turning the florets half way through**. Eat straight away.

# Easy eggs Florentine

In France, 'à la Florentine' means a dish served with spinach. Spinach tastes fantastic in this cheesy, white sauce. Baking eggs in the sauce make this a great special breakfast or light lunch.

## What you need
- 2 tbsp flour
- 2 tbsp vegetable oil
- 240ml (1 cup) milk
- 45g (½ cup) Cheddar cheese
- 4 child-sized handfuls spinach, washed
- 4 eggs

## Adult prep
- Preheat oven to 180°C/350°F/Gas 4.
- Grate the cheese.
- Lay out: ingredients, oven-proof dish, mixing spoon and small bowl or ramekin.

## How to make

**1** Put the flour and oil into the dish and mix them together.

**2** Put the milk, grated cheese and spinach in the dish and give it a good mix.

**3** Make four shallow gaps in the spinach mix for the eggs. Try to space them out.

**4** Break an egg into your small bowl or ramekin and then tip it into one of the gaps. Do this again with each egg.

Ask an adult to put the dish into the oven for 18 minutes.

**TOP TIP!**

Don't worry if your final sauce looks a bit lumpy. If you want a smoother sauce, do up to the end of Step 2 and ask an adult to help you heat the dish gently on a hob until it thickens. Then add the eggs and bake.

SERVES 2+2
ACTIVITY 15 min
18 min OVEN

## MAIN TASKS
- Mixing
- Breaking eggs

## ALLERGY INFO

| | |
|---|---|
| DAIRY | Use dairy-free milk |
| EGG | Leave out eggs to make creamy spinach |
| GLUTEN | Use gluten-free flour |
| NUT | Check labels |

# Pea green soup

The peas you often get as a vegetable on the side of your plate can be transformed into a delicious, hot soup. This soup is quick, bright, easy and lovely to dip fresh bread into.

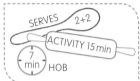

SERVES 2+2

ACTIVITY 15 min

7 min / HOB

## MAIN TASKS
- Tearing
- Mixing

## VARIATION
(v) Leave out the ham and use vegetable stock.

## ALLERGY INFO

| | |
|---|---|
| DAIRY | Make dairy-free pesto (recipe page 64) |
| EGG | No egg |
| GLUTEN | Use gluten-free bread |
| NUT | Make pesto without nuts (recipe page 64) |

## What you need
- 720ml (3 cups) chicken or vegetable stock
- 450g (3 cups) frozen peas
- 1 tbsp green pesto (recipe on page 64 or buy in jar)
- 4 slices of dried ham, such as serrano or Parma
- 6–8 fresh basil leaves

### Adult prep
- If not using liquid stock, make up the stock.
- Lay out: ingredients, pan and mixing spoon.

## TOP TIP!
I love crunching into whole peas, but if you prefer a smooth soup, ask an adult to blend to serve.

## How to make

1 Put the stock, peas and pesto into the pan and mix it all up.

2 Tear the ham into little bits and put the bits into the pan.

3 Tear the basil into little bits and put the bits into the pan.

4 Give the soup another mix.

Ask an adult to boil the soup on the hob for about 5 minutes or until the peas are cooked and the soup is piping hot..

# Potato patties

Burgers don't always need to have meat! You can serve this easy and tasty veggie burger as a main dish or on the side.

## What you need
- 400g baking potatoes
- 60g (⅓ cup) tinned sweetcorn
- 30g (⅓ cup) Cheddar cheese
- 4 chives
- 1 tbsp plain flour

## Adult prep
- Grate the cheese.
- Open and drain the sweetcorn.
- Bake the potatoes for 10 minutes in a microwave.
- Lay out: ingredients, table or child-safe knife, mixing bowl, metal spoon, child-safe scissors and plate or board.

### TOP TIP!
Don't worry too much about sticking to the amounts. Make these by eye and trust your own quantities.

## How to make

1 Chop the potatoes in half (2 bits).

2 Spoon or scrape the flesh out of each potato and put it into the bowl. (Don't throw away the potato skins – snip them up and ask an adult to bake them to make crisps.)

3 Put the sweetcorn and cheese into the bowl.

4 Snip the chives into little bits and put the bits into the bowl.

5 Squish and squash the mix with your hands until it is all mixed up.

6 Grab a handful of the mix and shape it into a ball.

7 Press down on the ball with a flat hand to make a burger shape.

8 Put the flour onto the plate or board and spread it out. Put the patty on the plate and then turn it over so a little bit of flour sticks to both sides.

9 Do Steps 6, 7 and 8 again until you have no mix left.

Ask an adult to fry the patties in a little oil for about 3 minutes each side until lightly browned.

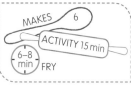

MAKES 6
ACTIVITY 15 min
6–8 min FRY

## MAIN TASKS
- Chopping
- Snipping
- Forming and shaping

## VARIATIONS
Make these as sausage rather than burger shapes. Or use up leftover cooked veggies by chopping them up and using instead of sweetcorn.

## ALLERGY INFO

| | |
|---|---|
| DAIRY | Use dairy-free cheese |
| EGG | No egg |
| GLUTEN | Use gluten-free flour |
| NUT | Check labels |

# Veggie muffins

You can use any vegetable to make these cheesy cakes. I've chosen asparagus because it's one of my favourites. Grated courgette or chopped cauliflower or broccoli also work well.

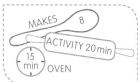

MAKES 8
ACTIVITY 20 min
15 min OVEN

## MAIN TASKS
- Egg breaking
- Mixing
- Snipping
- Spooning and scraping

## VARIATION
Tear up 3 slices of prosciutto or salami and add them to the mix.

## ALLERGY INFO

| | |
|---|---|
| DAIRY | Use dairy-free cheese |
| EGG | Avoid |
| GLUTEN | Use gluten-free flour |
| NUT | Check labels |

## TOP TIP!
Serve the muffins with the leftover asparagus and soup.

## What you need
- 1 egg
- 60ml (¼ cup) milk
- 2 tbsp olive oil
- 60ml (¼ cup) tomato soup
- 8 asparagus stalks
- 130g (1 cup) self-raising flour
- 50g (½ cup) Cheddar cheese

## Adult prep
- Preheat oven to 190°C/375°F/Gas 5.
- Open the tomato soup and pour into a bowl.
- Grate the cheese.
- Lay out: ingredients, mixing bowl, fork or hand whisk, child-safe scissors, spoon or spatula, 8 silicone cupcake cases and muffin or baking tray.

## How to make

1 Break the egg into the bowl.

2 Put the milk, olive oil and tomato soup into the bowl.

3 Whisk the mix with a fork or hand whisk.

4 Hold the bottom of each stalk of asparagus and bend the stalk until it breaks. Throw away the bit you were holding – this gets rid of the tough bits.

5 Snip or break the rest of the asparagus stalks into little bits and put them into the bowl.

6 Put the flour and cheese into the bowl.

7 Mix it all up.

8 Put the cupcake cases into a muffin tray or on a baking tray.

9 Spoon and scrape the mix into the cases. Try to get the same amount into each case.

Ask an adult to put the tray into the oven for 15 minutes or until the muffin tops feel springy when you touch them.

# Baba ganoush

This is a smoky, sweet Middle-Eastern dip made with baked aubergine. It's yummy scooped up with with baked or toasted pitta bread.

## What you need

- 1 aubergine
- 1 tbsp olive oil
- ¼ tsp ground cumin
- ⅛ tsp salt
- 2 tbsp single cream
- ¼ lemon
- ½ a garlic clove (optional)

## Adult prep

- Stab the aubergine a few times with a sharp knife and bake in a very hot oven for 20 minutes until tender inside. Leave to cool.
- Lay out: ingredients, table or child-safe knife, metal spoon, food processor and small bowl or pot with lid.

## How to make

**1** Chop the cooked aubergine in half.

**2** Scoop and scrape out the flesh of the aubergine.

**3** Put the aubergine flesh, olive oil, salt, cumin and cream into the food processor.

**4** Squeeze the lemon so the juice goes into the food processor.

**5** Chop the garlic clove in half (2 bits). Peel the skin off one bit and put it into the food processor.

**6** Whizz the mix up in the food processor until it looks smooth.

**7** Spoon and scrape the baba ganoush into a bowl or pot. Cover and keep in the fridge until ready to eat.

## TOP TIP!

The garlic gives it flavour, but also makes it taste sharp. If you prefer, you can use less garlic or leave it out. Experiment!

SERVES 4
ACTIVITY 15 min

## MAIN TASKS

- Chopping
- Peeling
- Using a food processor

## ALLERGY INFO

| | |
|---|---|
| DAIRY | Use dairy-free cream |
| EGG | No egg |
| GLUTEN | No gluten |
| NUT | Check labels |

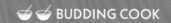 

# Flatbreads

You don't need to wait long for this bread to be ready. Make it plain or add different flavours like spices, cheese and herbs. You can even use these flatbreads as easy pizza bases.

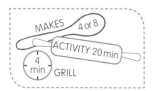

MAKES 4 or 8
ACTIVITY 20 min
4 min GRILL

## MAIN TASKS
- Mixing
- Kneading
- Forming and shaping
- Rolling

## VARIATION
Add ground cumin, crushed garlic or mixed herbs to the dough. Or add grated cheese and/or chopped chorizo, or a herb like rosemary or thyme.

## ALLERGY INFO

| | |
|---|---|
| DAIRY | Use dairy-free yoghurt |
| EGG | No egg |
| GLUTEN | Avoid |
| NUT | Check labels |

## What you need
- 250g (2 cups) self-raising flour
- 180g (¾ cup) Greek-style yoghurt
- ¼ tsp salt
- 1 tbsp plain flour for dusting
- 1 tbsp olive oil

## Adult prep
- Preheat the grill to hot.
- Lay out: ingredients, mixing bowl, mixing spoon, table or child-safe knife, rolling pin, pastry brush and baking tray.

### TOP TIP!
Unlike normal bread, you don't need to knead this dough for long – just enough to bring it together. If the dough is too dry, add a bit more yoghurt. If too wet, add a bit more flour.

## How to make

1 Put self-raising flour, yoghurt, salt and any additional flavour you want into the bowl and mix it all up.

2 Squish it with hands to make a ball of dough.

3 Dust the extra flour onto the work surface or table.

4 Put the dough onto the floured table and squish and squash (knead) it until it looks smooth.

5 Cut the dough into 4 bits (if you want large flatbreads) or 8 bits (if you want small flatbreads).

6 Roll each bit out flat.

7 Brush oil all over both sides of each bit.

8 Put the bits of dough onto the tray.

Ask an adult to put the flatbreads under the grill for about 2 minutes each side.

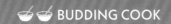
# Shortcrust pastry dough

If you can make shortcrust pastry, you can use it to make so many delicious things like quiches (page 62), pasties (page 98) and pies (pages 71 and 107).

## What you need
- 65g salted butter
- 135g (1 cup) plain flour
- 1 tbsp sugar (for sweet shortcrust only)
- 2 tbsp water

## Adult prep
Lay out: ingredients, chopping board, table or child-safe knife, mixing bowl and sheet of clingfilm.

## How to make

**1** Chop the butter into little bits and put them into the bowl.

**2** Put the flour (and sugar if making sweet shortcrust) into the bowl.

**3** Rub ('tickle') the butter bits into the flour using clean fingertips until the mix looks like breadcrumbs.

**4** Put the water in the bowl and use hands to mix and squish the pastry dough together into a ball.

**5** Wrap the ball in clingfilm and keep it in the fridge (up to 2 days) or freezer (up to a month) until ready to use. N.B. Let it return to room temperature before rolling out.

MAKES 220g
ACTIVITY 25 min

## MAIN TASKS
- Chopping
- 'Tickle fingers'
- Forming and shaping

## ALLERGY INFO

| | |
|---|---|
| DAIRY | Use dairy-free spread |
| EGG | No egg |
| GLUTEN | Can use gluten-free flour, but difficult because it tends to fall apart |
| NUT | Check labels |

**TOP TIP!**
Try not to squish and squash it too much, just enough to bring it together into a dough. If you work it too much, your pastry will go rubbery.

# Mini quiches

Spinach and red pepper make a yummy, colourful combination, but you can choose any veg you like. The size of these quiches make them great for a picnic or in a lunchbox.

MAKES 8
ACTIVITY 30 min
25 min
OVEN

## MAIN TASKS
- Dividing
- Dusting
- Rolling
- Chopping
- Breaking eggs
- Whisking
- Tearing

## ALLERGY INFO

| | |
|---|---|
| DAIRY | Use dairy-free pastry, dairy-free cream, leave out cheese |
| EGG | Avoid |
| GLUTEN | Use gluten-free pastry |
| NUT | Check labels |

## What you need
- 220g shortcrust pastry (shop-bought or recipe on page 61)
- 1 tbsp flour for dusting
- 2 eggs
- 60ml (¼ cup) single cream
- 30g (⅓ cup) Cheddar cheese
- ½ a red pepper
- 2 child-sized handfuls of washed baby spinach leaves

## Adult prep
- Preheat oven to 190°C/375°F/Gas 5.
- Grate the cheese.
- Lay out: ingredients, chopping board, rolling pin, table knife, flour for dusting, muffin tray, 8 bits of foil, mixing bowl and fork.

## How to make

**1** Cut the pastry into eighths (8 equal bits).

**2** Dust flour onto the board and rolling pin.

**3** Roll each bit of pastry flat into a circle or square.

**4** Put each bit of pastry into each hole in the muffin tray to make a cup shape.

**5** Put scrunched-up bits of foil in each pastry cup.

Ask an adult to put the muffin tray into the oven for 10 minutes. While the pastry is cooking …

**6** Break the eggs into the bowl.

**7** Put the cream in the bowl and whisk the mix with the fork.

**8** Pour the mix into each pastry cup.

**9** Pull the seeds and stalk off the pepper and wash it. Chop the red pepper into little bits.

**10** Tear the spinach leaves into bits.

**11** Put about the same amount of cheese, pepper and spinach bits into each pastry cup.

Ask an adult to put the muffin tray back into the oven for 15 minutes until the filling feels firm.

# Pesto

It's fun to grow the basil for this easy-to-make sauce. Use this pesto to add flavour to things like pasta, creamy sauces, breadcrumb crusts (page 87), soup (page 56) and bread (page 60).

MAKES 3 tbsp

ACTIVITY 15 min

## MAIN TASKS
- Peeling
- Using a food processor
- Spooning and scraping

## ALLERGY INFO

| | |
|---|---|
| DAIRY | Swap hard cheese for a handful of parsley |
| EGG | No egg |
| GLUTEN | No gluten |
| NUT | Swap pine nuts for a handful of parsley |

## TOP TIP!
Make a big batch in one go. You can store pesto in a clean, airtight jar in the fridge for about 5 days.

## What you need
- 1 garlic clove
- 2 tbsp pine nuts
- 20 large or 30 smaller basil leaves
- 20g (¼ cup) hard Italian cheese, such as Parmesan
- 2 tbsp olive oil

## Adult prep
- Finely grate the cheese (N.B. an older child could do this).
- Lay out: ingredients, rolling pin, food processor, spatula and jar or pot with a lid.

## How to make

1 Bash the garlic clove 1 or 2 times with a rolling pin to loosen the peel.

2 Take the peel off the garlic and put the peeled clove into the food processor.

3 Put the pine nuts, basil leaves, grated cheese and olive oil into the food processor.

4 Whizz up the mix in the processor until there are no whole pine nuts left.

5 Spoon and scrape the pesto into the jar.

6 Put on the lid and keep in the fridge until ready to use (see above for ideas).

# Red pepper hummus

You've probably had normal hummus lots of times, but this is a fun, brightly coloured alternative. Hummus is traditionally made with tahini, but I love it made with peanut butter.

## What you need
- 400g tinned chickpeas
- 60g roasted red pepper (buy in a jar)
- 1 tbsp peanut butter
- 1 tbsp olive oil
- ¼ tsp ground cumin
- ⅛ tsp salt
- ¼ lemon
- 1 garlic clove

## Adult prep
- Open the chickpea tin and empty the contents into a bowl but do not drain the liquid.
- Lay out: ingredients, mixing bowl, sieve or colander, food processor, rolling pin, pot with lid, spoon and spatula.

## How to make

**1** Put the sieve or colander over the bowl. Tip the chickpeas into the sieve. Keep the water from the chickpea tin in the bowl.

**2** Take off the sieve and put it under a cold tap to wash the chickpeas.

**3** Put the chickpeas into a food processor.

**4** Put 3 tbsp of the chickpea liquid from the bowl, the red pepper, peanut butter, olive oil, cumin and salt into the food processor.

**5** Squeeze the lemon so the juice goes into the food processor.

**6** Bash the clove of garlic with a rolling pin until the skin starts falling off. Peel the skin off and add the garlic to the food processor.

**7** Whizz the mix up in the food processor until it looks smooth. If it looks dry, add a bit more chickpea liquid.

**8** Spoon and scrape the hummus into a bowl or pot. Cover and keep in the fridge (up to 2 days) until ready to dip.

SERVES 4
ACTIVITY 15 min

## MAIN TASKS
- Peeling
- Using a food processor
- Spooning and scraping

## VARIATION
Leave out the red pepper for plain hummus.

## ALLERGY INFO

| DAIRY | No dairy |
| --- | --- |
| EGG | No egg |
| GLUTEN | No gluten |
| NUT | Avoid |

**TOP TIP!**

Snip pittas into strips with child-safe scissors. Ask an adult to bake the strips in a hot oven for 5 minutes until crispy – perfect for dipping into hummus or baba ganoush (page 59).

# Quesadillas

A quesadilla is a warm tortilla sandwich with melted cheese in the middle to help bind it together. Experiment with your own filling ideas.

MAKES 2
ACTIVITY 15 min
5 min FRY

## MAIN TASKS
- Flavour selection
- Chopping
- Snipping
- Mixing
- Brushing
- Spooning and scraping
- Spreading
- Using a hob

## VARIATION
Add a few spoonfuls of tinned sweetcorn instead of the tomatoes.

## ALLERGY INFO

| | |
|---|---|
| DAIRY | Leave out or use a vegan cheese |
| EGG | No egg |
| GLUTEN | Use gluten-free tortillas |
| NUT | Check labels |

## What you need
- 160g tinned tuna
- 30g (⅓ cup) Cheddar cheese
- 1 tbsp mayonnaise
- 3 cherry tomatoes
- 1 spring onion (optional)
- 2 tortillas
- 1 tsp oil

## Adult prep
- Open and drain the tin of tuna.
- Grate the cheese (an older child could do this).
- Be ready to help children fry quesadillas on the hob.
- Lay out: ingredients, mixing bowl, fork, mixing spoon, table or child-safe knife, child-safe scissors, pastry brush, frying pan, kitchen turner (flat spatula) and serving board or plate.

## How to make

**1** Put the tuna, cheese and mayonnaise into the bowl and mash with the fork.

**2** Chop or snip the tomatoes into into little bits and put them into the bowl.

**3** If using, snip the spring onion into little bits and put them into the bowl.

**4** Give it all a mix.

**5** Spoon and scrape the mix onto the tortillas and spread it out.

**6** Fold the tortillas in half.

**7** Brush the oil on both sides of the tortillas.

Ask an adult to help you put the pan onto a medium hob and help you fry the quesadillas.

**8** When the pan is hot, carefully put the tortillas in the pan. Do not touch the hot pan with your fingers.

**9** After 2 minutes, use the turner to turn the quesadillas over and fry the other side until golden brown and the cheese is melted. Turn off the hob.

**10** Use the turner to take the quesadillas out of the pan. Put them on the plate or board and slice.

 **CONFIDENT CHEF**

# Roots soup

Carrots and parsnips are root vegetables, which means they are the root of a plant (see page 118 for more info on types of veg). This soup is perfect with fresh bread on a cold winter's day.

## What you need
- 150g parsnips
- 450g carrots
- 4 shallots
- 2 garlic cloves
- 240ml (1 cup) coconut milk
- 240ml (1 cup) water
- 1 tsp garam masala
- ½ chicken or vegetable stock cube
- diced, cooked pancetta and croutons to garnish (optional)

## Adult prep
- Cut the root ends off the shallots.
- Be ready to help children use the microwave in Step 2.
- Lay out: ingredients, table or child-safe knife, chopping board, rolling pin and pan with lid.

## How to make

**1** Wash the parsnips and carrots in cold water.

**2** Put them into the microwave for 5 minutes to make them softer and easier to chop up.

**3** Chop the ends off the carrots and parsnips. Then chop them into big chunks. Put the chunks into the pan.

**4** Peel the shallots and put them into the pan.

**5** Bang the garlic cloves with the rolling pin until the skin starts coming off. Peel the skin off and put the peeled garlic into the pan.

**6** Put the coconut milk, water and garam masala into the pan.

**7** Rub ('tickle') the stock cube with fingertips over the pan so the bits go in.

**8** Put the lid on the pan.

Ask an adult to heat the pan on a hob for about 25 minutes (or until the vegetables are tender) and then blend the soup until it is smooth. If you like sprinkle on some diced cooked pancetta or croutons to serve.

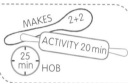

MAKES 2+2
ACTIVITY 20 min
25 min HOB

## MAIN TASKS
- Using a microwave
- Chopping
- Peeling
- 'Tickle fingers'

## ALLERGY INFO

| DAIRY | No dairy |
|-------|----------|
| EGG | No egg |
| GLUTEN | Check stock-cube label |
| NUT | Use water instead of coconut milk and check garam masala and stock-cube labels |

 **TOP TIP!**

Don't choose carrots and parsnips that are too thick – the thinner they are, the easier they are to chop.

# Friends for tea

One of the best things about cooking is making something to share. Family and friends will love these tasty snacks for playdates, parties or picnics. Or make up a batch for your own after-school nibbles.

 **EASY PEASY**

American-style cookies **70**

Chocolate chip mince pies **71**

Fairy cakes 5 ways **72**

  Victoria sponge **73**
  Lemon butterfly **73**
  Double chocolate **74**
  Vanilla **74**
  Christmas **74**

Tricolore sticks **75**

 **BUDDING COOK**

Aberffraw biscuits **76**

Fruit pops **77**

Sweet biscuits 5 ways **78**

  Ginger **79**
  Chocolate **79**
  Citrus **79**
  Vanilla **79**
  Thumb-print **79**

**CONFIDENT CHEF**

Rough puff straws **80**

Soda bread farls **81**

# American-style cookies

These soft, American biscuits full of chocolate chips make an easy, sweet tea-time treat.

MAKES 8
ACTIVITY 15 min
12 min OVEN

## MAIN TASKS
- Combining butter and sugar
- Breaking eggs
- Spooning and scraping
- Chopping

## VARIATIONS
Swap the chocolate chips for dried fruit like raisins or cranberries and add a pinch of cinnamon. Or swap chocolate chips for orange zest and chopped chocolate orange.

## ALLERGY INFO

| | |
|---|---|
| DAIRY | Swap butter for dairy-free spread and use dairy-free choc chips or dried fruit |
| EGG | Swap egg for 3 tbsp Greek-style yoghurt |
| GLUTEN | Use gluten-free flour |
| NUT | Check labels |

## What you need
- 55g butter
- 2 tbsp caster sugar
- 2 tbsp demerara sugar
- 1 egg
- 65g (½ cup) plain flour
- ⅛ tsp bicarbonate of soda
- 50g (¼ cup) chocolate chips

## Adult prep
- Take the butter out of the fridge well in advance to make sure it's soft.
- Preheat oven to 180°C/350°F/Gas 4.
- Lay out: ingredients, mixing bowl, wooden spoon, table knife, baking tray lined with baking paper or silicone mat, table spoon and spatula.

## How to make

1 Put the butter, caster sugar and demerara sugar into the bowl.

2 Use the spoon to squish and squash the sugar into the butter until it is all mixed in and the butter squishy.

3 Break the egg into the bowl and mix it into the butter and sugar mixture.

4 Put the flour, bicarbonate of soda and chocolate chips into the bowl and mix it all up.

5 Spoon and scrape 8 spoonfuls of cookie dough onto the baking tray. Make sure they are spaced out because they will spread in the oven.

Ask an adult to put the tray into the oven for 10 to 12 minutes until the cookies look golden but are still soft.

 **TOP TIP!**

Bake cookies to order when friends come over. Shape unbaked cookie dough into a large sausage, wrap it in clingfilm and put in the freezer. When you need cookies, cut slices off the sausage and bake them from frozen for 15 minutes.

# Chocolate chip mince pies

If you're not keen on the taste of mincemeat or you don't have time to make it, this is a delicious, instant alternative that's not just for Christmas.

## What you need

- 1 small apple
- 1 tbsp raisins
- 1 tbsp currants
- 1 tbsp dried cranberries
- 1 tbsp mixed peel
- 1 tbsp dark chocolate chips
- 1 tbsp golden syrup
- 220g shortcrust pastry
- 1 tbsp plain flour for dusting
- 1 tsp milk

## Adult prep

- Preheat oven to 200°C/390°F/Gas 6.
- Grate the apple, leaving out the core and pips (an older child could do this).
- Lay out: ingredients, mixing bowl, mixing spoon, rolling pin, 7 cm round cookie cutter, 4 or 5 cm star cookie cutter, 12-hole cupcake or shallow bun tray, pastry brush and teaspoon.

## How to make

1 Put the grated apple, raisins, currants, cranberries, mixed peel, chocolate chips and golden syrup into the bowl and mix it all up. Don't forget to make a wish as you stir!

2 Dust flour onto the worktop or table and then roll out the pastry.

3 Cut out 12 circles and 12 stars with the cookie cutters.

4 Put the circles into the holes in the tray.

5 Put a teaspoon of filling onto each circle.

6 Put a pastry star on top of each.

7 Brush a little milk on top of each pie.

Ask an adult to put the pies into the oven for 12 minutes.

**TOP TIP!**

These taste even better with home-made shortcrust pastry – recipe on page 61.

MAKES 12
ACTIVITY 25 min
12 min OVEN

## MAIN TASKS

- Dusting
- Rolling
- Cookie cutting
- Spooning and scraping
- Brushing

## VARIATION

Use mincemeat to make traditional mince pies.

## ALLERGY INFO

| DAIRY | Use dairy-free pastry and milk and check the chocolate chips |
| --- | --- |
| EGG | Check the pastry label if shop bought |
| GLUTEN | Use gluten-free pastry |
| NUT | Check labels |

# Fairy cakes 5 ways

Learn how to create your own fairy cake flavours with this basic recipe and ideas on how to change it into five different cakes. Choose one of these or come up with your own.

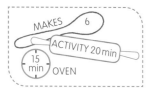

MAKES 6
ACTIVITY 20 min
15 min OVEN

## MAIN TASKS
- Flavour selection
- Breaking eggs
- Mixing
- Spooning and scraping
- Decorating

## ALLERGY INFO

| | |
|---|---|
| DAIRY | Use dairy-free spread |
| EGG | Use 2 tbsp of Greek-style yoghurt |
| GLUTEN | Use gluten-free flour |
| NUT | Check labels and choose version appropriately |

## What you need
- 55g (⅓ cup) caster sugar
- 55g butter
- 1 egg
- 65g (½ cup) self-raising flour
- 1 tbsp Greek-style yoghurt
- Your choice of flavour (see opposite for ideas)

## Adult prep
- Take the butter out of the fridge at least an hour before starting so it is soft.
- Preheat oven to 170°C/325°F/Gas 3
- Lay out: ingredients, mixing bowl, mixing spoon, 6 cupcake cases, cupcake tray and metal spoon or spatula.

## How to make

**1** Put the sugar and butter into the bowl and mix until they are mixed together.

**2** Break the egg into the bowl and mix.

**3** Put the flour and yoghurt into the bowl and mix it all up.

**4** Put in the flavour you have chosen (see opposite for ideas) and mix.

**5** Put the cupcake cases into the tray.

**6** Spoon and scrape the mixture into each cupcake case. Make sure each one has the same amount.

Ask an adult to put the cakes into the oven for 15 minutes until the tops feel springy to touch. Leave them to cool before decorating.

### TOP TIP!

The softer the butter, the easier it is to mix. If it is too hard, put it in the microwave on 30 per cent power for 30 seconds. Keep doing that until you can squish with your finger. But be careful, you must not melt it!

# 1 Victoria sponge

**What you need**

- 2 tbsp strawberry or raspberry jam
- 1 tbsp icing sugar
- table or child-safe knife
- a sieve

**How to make**

1 Bake the cakes without adding flavour (no Step 4).

2 Cut the cakes in half horizontally so you have two circles.

3 Spread strawberry or raspberry jam on one of the circles.

4 Put the other circle on top like a sandwich.

5 Dust the tops with icing sugar.

# 2 Lemon butterfly

**What you need**

- zest of ½ a lemon
- 2 tbsp icing sugar, plus a little for dusting
- 1 tbsp lemon curd
- a small mixing bowl
- a mixing spoon
- table or child-safe knife
- a sieve

**How to make**

1 Follow the basic recipe and add lemon zest in Step 4.

2 When baked and cool, cut off the tops of the cakes so you have flat-topped cakes and a small circle of cake.

3 Cut each small circle that came off the tops in half to make two semicircles. Then trim these slightly to make them look like butterfly wings.

4 Mix the icing sugar and lemon curd in the bowl until it is smooth.

5 Dollop a bit of lemon icing on top of each cake.

6 Put the butterfly wing cake bits into the curd to look like a butterfly.

7 Dust the tops with icing sugar.

### 3 Double chocolate

**What you need**
- 2 tbsp cocoa powder
- 3 tbsp chocolate chips
- 1 tbsp Greek-style yoghurt
- 3 tbsp chocolate spread
- chocolate Buttons, Maltesers or chocolate sprinkles to decorate.

**How to make**

1 Follow the basic recipe and put in the cocoa powder, chocolate chips and 1 tbsp extra of yoghurt in Step 4.

2 When baked and cool, spread ½ tbsp of chocolate spread onto each cake and decorate.

### 4 Vanilla

**What you need**
- 1 tsp vanilla extract (½ tsp for cakes, ½ tsp for icing)
- 40g soft butter
- 130g (1 cup) icing sugar
- 1 tbsp milk
- coloured sweets or sprinkles to decorate
- electric whisk
- bowl
- table or palette knife

**How to make**

1 Follow the basic recipe and put in ½ tsp vanilla extract in Step 4.

2 When the cakes are baked and cool, use an electric whisk to mix up the butter, icing sugar, ½ tsp vanilla extract and milk until it is fluffy. This is called buttercream.

3 Spread the vanilla buttercream onto the cakes and decorate.

### 5 Christmas

**What you need**
- 1 tsp mixed spice
- 3 tbsp mixed peel
- 4 tbsp icing sugar
- 1½ tsp water
- sprinkles or Christmas cake decorations
- a small mixing bowl
- mixing spoon

**How to make**

1 Follow the basic recipe and put in the mixed spice and mixed peel in Step 4.

2 When the cakes are baked and cool, put the icing sugar and water into the bowl and mix until it looks smooth. If it looks thin, add a little more icing sugar. If it looks too thick, add a tiny bit more water.

3 Spoon the icing onto the baked cakes and decorate.

# Tricolore sticks

These colourful, quick, healthy snacks are munched off a stick. They are in the green, white and red of the Italian flag, which is called the 'tricolore'.

## What you need
- 1 ripe avocado
- 220g (125g drained) mozzarella cheese
- 12 cherry tomatoes
- 24 cocktail sticks

## Adult prep
- Cut the avocado in half, leave the stone in and put it back together (this delays the flesh turning brown).
- Lay out: ingredients, spoon, table or child-safe knife and chopping board.

## How to make

1 Peel the thick skin off the avocado and scoop out the stone with a spoon.

2 Chop the avocado and mozzarella cheese into chunks about 1 cm by 1 cm.

3 Chop the tomatoes in half.

4 Spike one of the avocado chunks with the stick and slide it up the stick.

5 Spike a mozzarella chunk and slide it up.

6 Finally, spike a tomato chunk.

7 Eat straight away or cover and eat within an hour.

MAKES 24

ACTIVITY 15 min

## MAIN TASKS
- Peeling
- Chopping
- Threading on skewers

## VARIATIONS
Swap the avocado for basil leaves or do a fruity version with strawberries, banana and grapes

## ALLERGY INFO

| DAIRY | Use tinned pineapple chunks instead of cheese |
|---|---|
| EGG | No egg |
| GLUTEN | No gluten |
| NUT | Check labels |

## TOP TIP!

Make sure the avocado is ripe, otherwise it will be difficult to peel. Test the ripeness by gently pressing the top. If it feels hard, it isn't ripe. If it feels soft, it is ripe. If it feels really squishy, it is too ripe.

# Aberffraw biscuits

Aberffraw biscuits are named after the place in Wales where they were first made. They are usually shaped using scallop shells, but you can mould them into any silicone moulds you have.

MAKES 12
ACTIVITY 15 min
15 min OVEN

## MAIN TASKS
- Using a microwave
- Mixing
- Decorating

## ALLERGY INFO

| | |
|---|---|
| DAIRY | Swap butter for dairy-free spread |
| EGG | No egg |
| GLUTEN | Use gluten-free flour (N.B. it doesn't bind as well so use simple moulds) |
| NUT | Check labels |

**TOP TIP!**
Add food colouring to the dough to make the biscuits in fun colours.

## What you need
- 60g butter
- 3 tbsp caster sugar
- 130g (1 cup) plain flour
- icing pens or tubes for decorating (optional)

## Adult prep
- Preheat oven to 180°C/350°F/Gas 4.
- Be ready to help the children use the microwave in Step 1.
- Lay out: ingredients, microwave-safe bowl, mixing spoon and oven-safe silicone moulds or cases.

## How to make

1 Put the butter into the bowl and put it in the microwave for 30 seconds or until the butter has melted.

2 Put the sugar into the bowl and mix.

3 Add the flour into the bowl and mix again to make a dough.

4 Squish dough into each mould or case. Make sure you press it well into the corners.

Ask an adult to put the biscuits into the oven for 15 minutes (longer if using large moulds, shorter for smaller ones).

5 When the biscuits are baked and cool, take them out of the moulds and decorate.

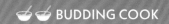
# Fruit pops

What could be nicer than fresh fruit dipped in chocolate and sprinkles on a stick? Be warned, they disappear fast!

## What you need

- 1 easy peeler orange or tangerine
- 10 small or strawberries or 5 large strawberries, halved
- 1 cardboard box, e.g. a cereal box
- 20 cocktail sticks
- 25g (3 segments) chocolate orange
- 1 tbsp sprinkles
- 25g milk chocolate

## Adult prep

- Be ready to help children use the microwave in Step 5.
- Lay out: ingredients, 2 microwave-safe bowls, 2 mixing spoons, a small bowl, a table or child-safe knife and a chopping board.

## How to make

**1** Peel the orange and pull apart all the segments.

**2** Chop the green bits (hulls) off the strawberries.

**3** Put the sprinkles into the small bowl.

**4** Lay the cereal box on its side and use a cocktail stick to make 20 holes on the top part. Make sure you space them out.

**5** Put the chocolate orange segments into a microwave-safe bowl and microwave them for 1 minute on 30 per cent power. Mix the chocolate until it melts. If it isn't melted, put it back in the microwave for 30 seconds on 30 per cent power.

**6** Dip the orange segments into the melted chocolate orange and then into the sprinkles.

**7** Put the decorated segments onto cocktail sticks and put the sticks into the holes in the cereal box.

**8** Melt the milk chocolate in the microwave in the same way as in Step 5.

**9** Make the strawberry pops in the same way as the orange ones. Put them on cocktail sticks and stick into the remaining holes in the cereal box.

**10** Put the cereal box with all the pops sticking out on top into the fridge until the chocolate sets.

MAKES 20
ACTIVITY 20 min
30 min CHILL

## MAIN TASKS

- Peeling
- Chopping
- Threading on a skewer
- Using a microwave
- Sprinkling

## VARIATION

Chopped banana also works well.

## ALLERGY INFO

| DAIRY | Use dairy-free dark chocolate (check the label) |
| --- | --- |
| EGG | No egg |
| GLUTEN | No gluten |
| NUT | Check labels |

 **TOP TIP!**

You must melt chocolate low and slow. If you use too much heat, the chocolate will go greasy and grainy.

# Sweet biscuits 5 ways

Basic ingredients in a sweet biscuit are flour, butter and sugar. Beyond that, you can add anything you like to make different flavours. Opposite are some options, but make up your own too!

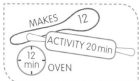

MAKES 12
ACTIVITY 20 min
12 min OVEN

## MAIN TASKS
- Flavour selection
- Combining butter and sugar
- Forming and shaping
- Rolling
- Cookie cutting
- Decorating

## ALLERGY INFO

| | |
|---|---|
| DAIRY | Use dairy-free spread |
| EGG | No egg |
| GLUTEN | Use gluten-free flour |
| NUT | Check labels |

## What you need
- 70g butter
- 3 tbsp sugar (caster or light brown)
- 130g (1 cup) plain flour

## Adult prep
- Take the butter out of the fridge at least an hour before starting so it is soft.
- Preheat oven to 180C/350F/Gas 4.
- Lay out: ingredients, mixing bowl, wooden spoon, rolling pin, 2 sheets of clingfilm, cookie cutters and lined baking tray.

## How to make

**1** Put the butter and sugar into the bowl and squish and squash with the spoon until they are mixed together.

**2** If adding another flavour, put the ingredients into the bowl and mix (see the next page for some options).

**3** Put the flour into the bowl and mix. As the mix starts to come together, use your hands to squish it together into a ball of dough.

**4** Put a sheet of clingfilm on the worktop or table. Put the dough on top and press flat with hands.

**5** Put another sheet of clingfilm on the dough and then roll the dough out between the clingfilm sheets. If you don't have clingfilm or the dough is sticky, dust the rolling area with a bit of flour.

**6** Remove the top sheet of clingfilm and cut out shapes with cookie cutters. Put the shapes onto a baking tray lined with baking paper or a baking mat.

Ask an adult to put the biscuits into the oven for 12 minutes until light brown. Leave for a minute on the tray then transfer them to a cooling rack to cool. Store in an airtight container.

## 1 Ginger

**What you need**
- ¼ banana
- 1 tsp ground ginger
- a fork
- a small plate
- writing icing tubes (optional)

### How to make

1 Mash the banana on the plate with a fork.

2 Make the biscuits using light brown sugar rather than caster sugar and put in the mashed banana and ginger at Step 2.

3 Once baked and cool, decorate the biscuits with whatever you like. I usually use writing icing, which comes in easy-to-use tubes.

## 2 Chocolate

**What you need**
- 2 tbsp cocoa powder
- ½ a small avocado
- a metal spoon
- a fork
- a small plate

### How to make

1 Peel the avocado and scrape out the flesh.

2 Mash the avocado on the plate with a fork.

3 Make the biscuits and put in 1 tbsp mashed avocado and the cocoa powder at Step 2.

## 3 Citrus

**What you need**
- ½ lemon or small orange
- a zester
- a juicer
- 1 tbsp icing sugar
- a sieve

### How to make

1 Scrape the zest off the lemon or orange.

2 Squeeze some juice from the lemon or orange

3 Make the biscuits and put in 1 tsp of the juice and the zest at Step 2.

4 Once baked and cool, dust the biscuits with icing sugar.

## 4 Vanilla

**What you need**
- ½ tsp vanilla extract
- writing icing tubes (optional)

### How to make

1 Make the biscuits and put in the vanilla extract at Step 2.

2 Once baked and cool, decorate the biscuits with whatever you like. I usually use writing icing, which comes in easy-to-use tubes.

## 5 Thumb-print

**What you need**
- 1 tsp water
- 2 tbsp jam
- a teaspoon

### How to make

1 Make the biscuit dough up to Step 3, putting in the water at Step 2.

2 Instead of rolling and cutting, take lumps of dough and shape them into balls.

3 Put the balls onto the baking tray and flatten them with a flat hand.

4 Use a thumb to make a dent in the middle of the biscuits.

5 Fill the dents with spoonfuls of jam, then bake.

 CONFIDENT CHEF

# Rough puff straws

Rough puff pastry isn't as puffy as puff pastry, but it's much easier to make and you can use it to make all sorts of tarts (page 104) and pies. These straws are great for snacking or in lunchboxes.

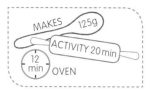

MAKES 125g

ACTIVITY 20 min

12 min OVEN

## MAIN TASKS
- Flavour selection
- 'Tickle fingers'
- Dusting
- Rolling
- Sprinkling

## VARIATION
Top your straws with whatever seed, herb, cheese or other topping you like.

## ALLERGY INFO

| | |
|---|---|
| DAIRY | Swap butter for dairy-free spread, avoid cheese as a topping |
| EGG | No egg |
| GLUTEN | Buy gluten-free puff pastry and start from Step 9 |
| NUT | Check labels |

## What you need
- 65g cold salted butter
- 65g (½ cup) plain flour
- 1 tsp water
- extra flour for dusting
- 1–2 tbsp topping e.g. poppy seeds or grated Parmesan

## Adult prep
- Preheat oven to 200°C/390°F/Gas 6.
- Lay out: ingredients, mixing bowl, table or child-safe knife, chopping board, rolling pin, baking tray lined with greaseproof paper or baking mat.

### TOP TIP!
Rough puff pastry works best when the butter is cold. So use butter from the fridge and if you have time, wrap your pastry in clingfilm and chill it in the fridge for 15 minutes between folds.

## How to make

**1** Cut the butter into little bits. Put the bits into the bowl.

**2** Put the flour into the bowl and rub ('tickle') the butter into the flour using fingertips.

**3** Put the water into the bowl and squish the mix together with hands to make a dough.

**4** Dust a little flour onto the worktop and rolling pin. Roll the dough out into a long rectangle.

**5** Fold the rectangle in half and then in half again.

**6** Turn the folded rectangle by one quarter (like turning a clock hand from quarter-to to o'clock).

**7** Roll the dough out into a long rectangle again.

**8** Fold the rectangle in half and then in half again.

**9** Roll the pastry out into a square.

**10** Sprinkle on your chosen topping and gently squash it into the pastry to stop it falling off.

**11** Cut the pastry into 1 cm strips and carefully lay them on the baking tray.

Ask an adult to put the straws into the oven for 10 minutes until crispy. Leave to cool.

# Soda bread farls

A super-quick, traditional Irish bread cut into quarters ('farl' means quarter). It's a great starter recipe for frying as it is done on a low heat with no oil.

## What you need

- 100g (⅔ cup) plain or wholemeal flour, plus extra for dusting
- 25g (¼ cup) oats
- ¼ tsp bicarbonate of soda
- ⅛ tsp salt
- 80g (⅓ cup) Greek-style yoghurt
- 2 tbsp milk

## Adult prep

- Lay out: ingredients, mixing bowl, mixing spoon, table or child-safe knife, frying pan, kitchen turner (flat spatula), serving plate
- Be on hand to supervise the dry frying of the farls.

## How to make

**1** Put the flour, oats, bicarbonate of soda, salt, yoghurt and milk into the bowl.

**2** Mix it all up and use your hands to squish it together into a ball of dough.

**3** Dust some flour onto the worktop or table. Put the dough on top and squish and squash (knead) it.

**4** Shape the dough with hands into a flat circle about 1 cm high.

**5** Use the table or child-safe knife to cut the circle into quarters (farls).

Ask an adult to help you put the frying pan onto a medium to low heat hob to cook the farls.

**6** Wait a few minutes until the pan is warm. Carefully put the farls into the pan. Be careful not to touch the pan – it will be hot.

**7** After about 6 minutes, use the turner to carefully turn the farls over and cook for another 6 minutes. Turn off the hob.

**8** Carefully lift the farls off the pan and put on a plate. Cut through the middle and spread with butter and jam or honey.

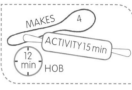

MAKES 4
ACTIVITY 15 min
12 min HOB

## MAIN TASKS

- Forming and shaping
- Kneading
- Dividing
- Using a hob

## ALLERGY INFO

| | |
|---|---|
| DAIRY | Use dairy-free milk and yoghurt |
| EGG | No egg |
| GLUTEN | Use gluten-free flour and oats |
| NUT | Check labels |

**TOP TIP!**

Soda bread isn't like normal bread and you don't need to knead it much – just enough to get the dough together.

# Family supper

The ultimate head-chef challenge: cooking dinner for the family. These yummy dishes from around the world will make it easy and fun with plenty of scope for children to get creative and make them their own.

# Cheeseburgers

These easy-to-make burgers are so yummy you may never want to eat shop-bought ones again!

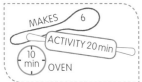

MAKES 6
ACTIVITY 20 min
10 min OVEN

## MAIN TASKS

- Handling raw meat
- Egg breaking
- Snipping
- Forming and shaping

## VARIATIONS

Try also making the basic bread rolls on page 50 to put the burgers in.
(v) Use the potato patties (page 57).

## ALLERGY INFO

| DAIRY | Leave out the cheese |
|---|---|
| EGG | Leave out the egg |
| GLUTEN | Leave out the egg and breadcrumbs |
| NUT | Check labels |

## What you need

- 500g minced beef
- ⅛ tsp salt
- 8 grinds of black pepper
- 30g fresh breadcrumbs (1 slice of bread whizzed in a food processor)
- 1 egg
- a handful of fresh parsley
- 6 thin slices of cheese

## Adult prep

- Preheat oven to 200°C/390°F/Gas 6.
- Lay out: ingredients, mixing bowl, child-safe scissors, cup, baking tray and sheet of foil.

**TOP TIP!**

Squish the mixture through your fingers lots of times because it helps mix the ingredients in and make the meat more tender.

## How to make

**1** Put the mince, salt, pepper and breadcrumbs in the bowl.

**2** Break the egg into the bowl.

**3** Put the parsley into the cup and use child-safe scissors to snip it into little bits.

**4** Tip the parsley bits into the bowl.

**5** Put the sheet of foil on the baking tray.

**6** Use your hands to squish and squash the mixture until everything is mixed together.

**7** Grab a handful of the mixture (about a sixth) and shape it into a ball.

**8** Put the ball onto the tray and use your hand to flatten it until it looks like a burger.

**9** Keep making burgers until you have made six. Make sure the burgers are about the same size and height. You can take bits from others to even them out. Don't forget to wash your hands after touching raw meat.

Ask an adult to put the tray into the oven for 10 to 15 minutes. Put a slice of cheese on top of each burger while they are still hot.

# Chunky chowder

Popular on both coasts of the USA, chowder is a delicious, creamy soup-like stew, usually made with fish or seafood.

## What you need

- 1 tbsp plain flour
- 1 tbsp vegetable oil
- 480g (2 cups) milk
- 240ml (1 cup) water
- 1 fish stock cube
- 4 slices of prosciutto (optional)
- 350g cauliflower (approx ½ head)
- 4 frozen smoked haddock fillets
- 150g (1 cup) frozen peas
- 150g (1 cup) frozen or tinned sweetcorn
- 4 tbsp dried fried onions
- a handful of fresh parsley

## Adult prep

Lay out: ingredients, pan with lid, mixing spoon, child-safe scissors and cup.

## How to make

**1** Put the flour and oil into the pan and mix them together.

**2** Add the milk and water into the pan and mix well.

**3** Rub ('tickle') the stock cube in your fingertips over the pan so the bits go in.

**4** If using, tear the prosciutto into the little bits and put them into the pan.

**5** Break the cauliflower into little bits and put the bits into the pan.

**6** Put the fish, peas, sweetcorn and dried onions into the pan.

**7** Put the parsley into the cup and snip it into small bits. Tip the bits into the pan.

**8** Give it all a good mix and put the lid on the pan.

Ask an adult to put the pan onto the hob and simmer gently for 20 minutes or until the fish is soft and flaky. Serve with fresh bread.

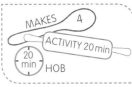

MAKES 4
ACTIVITY 20 min
20 min
HOB

## MAIN TASKS

- Mixing
- 'Tickle fingers'
- Tearing
- Handling fish (optional)
- Snipping

## VARIATIONS

Use other fish like cod or hake or seafood like tinned clams. Swap any of the vegetables for other veg like broccoli or French beans. **(v)** Swap fish for 350g broccoli and leave out the prosciutto.

## ALLERGY INFO

| | |
|---|---|
| DAIRY | Use dairy-free milk |
| EGG | No egg |
| GLUTEN | Use gluten-free flour and check the stock-cube label |
| NUT | Check labels |

# Creamy veg pasta bake

This creamy, cheesy pasta bake should be a hit with the whole family. It's easy to make, will fill you up quickly and is perfect for an active day when you need lots of energy.

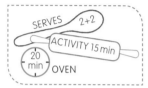

SERVES 2+2

ACTIVITY 15 min

20 min OVEN

## MAIN TASKS
- Whisking
- Mixing
- Snipping
- Sprinkling

## VARIATIONS
Swap peas for another veg like grated courgette or use a mix of two. Add 65g (½ cup) smoked diced pancetta.

## ALLERGY INFO

| | |
|---|---|
| DAIRY | Use dairy-free cream cheese, swap crème fraîche and milk for dairy-free cream and leave out hard cheese |
| EGG | Make sure pasta is egg-free |
| GLUTEN | Use gluten-free pasta |
| NUT | Check labels |

## What you need
- 120g (½ cup) cream cheese
- 120g (½ cup) crème fraîche
- 60ml (¼ cup) milk
- 6 chives
- 250g (2 cups) frozen peas
- ⅛ tsp salt
- 8 grinds of black pepper
- 350g fresh fusilli or penne pasta (or 225g dried, par-boiled for 5 minutes and chilled)
- 20g (⅓ cup) Italian hard cheese, such as Parmesan

### Adult prep
- Preheat oven to 190°C/375°F/Gas 5.
- Finely grate the hard cheese (an older child could do this).
- Lay out: ingredients, mixing bowl, whisk, child-safe scissors, mixing spoon and oven-proof dish.

## How to make

1 Put the cream cheese, crème fraîche and milk into the bowl. Whisk them together until smooth.

2 Use the scissors to snip the chives into little bits, the smaller the better. Put the bits into the bowl.

3 Put the peas, salt, pepper and pasta into the bowl. Mix it all together.

4 Put the mixture into the baking dish and spread it out until it is flat.

5 Sprinkle the grated cheese over the top.

Ask an adult to put the dish into the oven for 20 minutes.

### TOP TIP!
You can make this as a pasta sauce instead of a bake by heating everything except the pasta on a hob until the peas are cooked. Stir the sauce through your drained pasta.

# Crunchy pesto fish

Fish with breadcrumbs is a classic. This easy pesto and breadcrumb topping turns even the most boring fish into a delicious, crunchy feast.

## What you need
- 30g (⅔ cup) wholemeal breadcrumbs (1 slice of bread whizzed in a food processor)
- 2 tbsp green pesto (shop-bought or recipe on page 64)
- 1 tsp olive oil for greasing
- 4 boneless fresh fish fillets

## Adult prep
- Preheat oven to 200°C/390°F/Gas 6.
- Lay out: ingredients, mixing bowl, mixing spoon, pastry brush and baking tray.

### TOP TIP!
Line the baking tray with a sheet of foil, shiny-side up, to stop the fish sticking. And put the fish on the tray skin-side down so even if it does stick, the fish stays intact.

## How to make

1 Put the breadcrumbs and pesto into the bowl. Mix them up until the breadcrumbs are green.

2 Brush oil all over the baking tray.

3 Put the fish onto the tray skin-side down.

4 Use your hands to put the pesto breadcrumbs on the fish. Try to cover as much of the fish as possible.

Ask an adult to put the fish into the oven for 10 minutes for a slim fish like plaice or about 15 minutes for a thicker fish like cod, hake or salmon. Check the middle of the fillet with a knife – if the fish flakes easily, it is cooked.

SERVES 4
ACTIVITY 15 min
10–15 min OVEN

## MAIN TASKS
- Mixing
- Brushing
- Handling fish

## VARIATION
Use any fish you like. My favourite is plaice. **(v)** Bake the crunchy topping on its own and sprinkle onto salad to make it more exciting.

## ALLERGY INFO

| | |
|---|---|
| DAIRY | Make pesto without cheese (see page 64) |
| EGG | No egg |
| GLUTEN | Use gluten-free breadcrumbs |
| NUT | Make pesto without nuts (see page 64) |

# Minty lamb pittas

Lamb burgers or kebabs served with pittas make a yummy change from beef burgers. These go great with the Mediterranean kebabs on page 93.

MAKES 6–8

ACTIVITY 20 min

20 min

OVEN

## MAIN TASKS
• Chopping
• Forming and shaping
• Handling raw meat

## VARIATIONS
**(v)** Make the potato patties (page 57) or Mediterranean kebabs (page 93)

## ALLERGY INFO

| | |
|---|---|
| DAIRY | Leave out the halloumi |
| EGG | No egg |
| GLUTEN | Leave out pittas |
| NUT | Check labels |

## What you need
• 40g halloumi cheese
• 500g minced lamb
• 2 tbsp tinned tomatoes or passata
• 2 tsp dried mint
• ⅛ lemon
• 6 small pittas

## Adult prep
• Preheat oven to 200°C/390°F/Gas 6
• Lay out: ingredients, table knife, chopping board, mixing bowl, baking tray lined with a sheet of foil and 8 kebab sticks (optional)

### TOP TIP!
Make these about an hour before you need to cook them and put them in the fridge. Chilling helps them keep their shape when cooking, especially on a BBQ.

## How to make

**1** Chop the halloumi into tiny bits, the smaller the better.

**2** Put the chopped halloumi, lamb mince, tomatoes and dried mint into the bowl.

**3** Squeeze the bit of lemon so the juice goes into the bowl.

**4** Squish and squash the mix with hands until everything is mixed together.

**5** Grab a handful of mixture and shape it into a burger or sausage shape.

**6** If doing kebabs, mould the sausages around the kebab stick or skewer.

**7** Keep making burgers or kebabs until you have no mixture left. Make sure they are all about the same size and height.

**8** Put the burgers or kebabs on the lined baking tray. Wash your hands after handling the raw meat.

Ask an adult to put them into the oven for 20 minutes, turning halfway through. Ask them to heat the pittas then open them and put the lamb inside to serve.

# One-pot Bolognese rice

If you love a spag bol, try this easy, one-pot dish to make a change. Serve on its own or use to stuff marrow or red pepper (stuff, sprinkle with cheese and bake).

## What you need

- 350g beef mince
- 1 tbsp tomato paste
- 1 tbsp onion granules or powder
- 1 x 400g tin of chopped tomatoes
- ½ tbsp mixed dried herbs or a handful of chopped fresh herbs
- 140g (¾ cup) brown or wholemeal rice
- 180ml (¾ cup) water
- ½ beef or chicken stock cube
- 4 savoy cabbage leaves
- 1 garlic clove
- 2 tbsp grated cheese (optional)

## Adult prep

- Open the tin of tomatoes and empty contents into a bowl.
- Lay out: ingredients, large pan with lid, rolling pin, table (or child-safe) knife, chopping board, garlic press and mixing spoon.

## How to make

1 Put the mince, tomato paste, onion granules, chopped tomatoes, herbs, rice and water into the pan.

2 Rub ('tickle') the stock cube with your fingertips over the pan so the bits go in.

3 Tear the cabbage leaves into small bits and put them into the pan.

4 Bash the garlic with a rolling pin until the skin is loose. Peel the garlic and crush it through a garlic press. Put the crushed garlic into the pan.

5 Give it all a good mix and put the lid on.

Ask an adult to **put the pan on a low to medium heat on the hob for 50 minutes until the rice is cooked through.** If using, sprinkle on some grated cheese to serve.

**TOP TIP!**

If you want to make Bolognese sauce for some spaghetti, just leave out the rice and water.

SERVES 2+2
ACTIVITY 20 min
50 min HOB

## MAIN TASKS

- Handing raw meat
- 'Tickle fingers'
- Tearing
- Peeling
- Mixing

## VARIATIONS

Swap cabbage for any vegetable you like – spinach, red pepper or courgette work well. **(v)** Use Quorn mince and a vegetable stock cube.

## ALLERGY INFO

| DAIRY | Leave out cheese |
| --- | --- |
| EGG | No egg |
| GLUTEN | Check stock cube is gluten-free |
| NUT | Check labels |

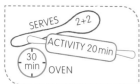

# Chickadee frickadee

A fricassée is a French dish, which is a stew with a white sauce. My daughter calls it chickadee frickadee and the name has stuck. It's a great way to use up leftover chicken or turkey after a roast.

SERVES 2+2

ACTIVITY 20 min

30 min

OVEN

## MAIN TASKS
- Mixing
- Chopping
- Whisking
- Tearing
- Sprinkling

## VARIATIONS
Swap the sweetcorn or celery for veg like peas or chopped carrots.
**(v)** Swap chicken for cooked or tinned potatoes, add some grated cheese to the breadcrumb topping and use vegetable stock.

## ALLERGY INFO

| DAIRY | Use dairy-free milk |
|---|---|
| EGG | No egg |
| GLUTEN | Use gluten-free flour and gluten-free breadcrumbs |
| NUT | Check labels |

## What you need
- 4 tbsp plain flour
- 4 tbsp vegetable oil
- 240ml (1 cup) chicken stock
- 240ml (1 cup) milk
- 1 stick of celery
- 300g (2 cups) cooked chicken
- 60g (1 cup) tinned sweetcorn
- 30g (⅔ cup) frozen wholemeal breadcrumbs (1 slice of frozen bread whizzed in a food processor)

## Adult prep
- Preheat oven to 190°C/375°F/Gas 5.
- Open the sweetcorn tin.
- Make up a cup of chicken stock.
- Lay out: ingredients, oven-proof dish, mixing spoon, child-safe or table knife and chopping board.

## How to make

**1** Put the flour and oil into the dish and mix them together.

**2** Put the stock and milk into the dish and mix it all up.

**3** Chop the celery into little bits, the smaller the better, and put them into the dish.

**4** Tear the chicken into bite-sized pieces and put them into the dish

**5** Tip and use the spoon to scrape the sweetcorn out of the tin and into the dish. Never put your hands inside a tin.

**6** Mix it all up.

**7** Sprinkle the breadcrumbs all over the top.

Ask an adult to put the dish into the oven for 30 minutes.

### TOP TIP!
If you're not keen on celery, keep it in anyway. Cooked celery is a magic ingredient: you can't really taste it but it makes the whole dish fresher and tastier when it's there.

# Chocolate chilli

This mild, full-of-flavour chilli has a 'secret' ingredient. See if anyone can guess you put chocolate in!

## What you need
- 500g diced beef
- 1 x 400g tin kidney beans
- 1 red pepper
- 1 x 400g tin of chopped tomatoes
- 1 x 400g tin of chicken or vegetable broth
- 1 tsp cumin
- ½ tsp cinnamon
- ⅛ tsp chilli powder
- 2 cloves of garlic
- 2 tbsp dark chocolate chips
- ½ a lime

## Adult prep
- Preheat oven to 150°C/300°F/Gas 2.
- Cut the pepper in half.
- Open all the tins.
- Lay out: ingredients, large oven-proof dish or pan with lid, sieve, mixing spoon, table or child-safe knife, chopping board and rolling pin.

## How to make

**1** Put the beef into the dish.

**2** Tip the kidney beans into the sieve. Use a spoon (not your hand) to scrape out any beans left in the tin.

**3** Hold the sieve under a cold tap to wash the beans. Put the washed beans into the dish.

**4** Pull the stalk off of the pepper and wash it under a cold tap to get rid of all the seeds.

**5** Chop the washed pepper into small chunks and put them into the dish.

**6** Put the tomatoes, broth, cumin, cinnamon and chilli powder into the dish. Wash your hands after touching chilli and do not touch your face until then.

**7** Bash the garlic cloves with a rolling pin. Take off the skin and put the peeled garlic into the dish.

**8** Give it all a good mix and put on the lid.

Ask an adult to put the chilli into the oven for 1½ to 2 hours until the meat is soft.

**9** When out of the oven and still hot, mix in the chocolate chips and juice from the lime. Serve with rice or in tacos with sour cream, guacamole and grated cheese.

SERVES 4
ACTIVITY 25 min
2 hrs OVEN

## MAIN TASKS
- Handing raw meat
- Chopping
- Peeling
- Mixing

## VARIATION
Add extra veg like spinach or courgette. **(v)** Use Quorn mince and cook for 1 hour.

## ALLERGY INFO

| DAIRY | Check the dark chocolate label or leave out the chocolate |
|---|---|
| EGG | No egg |
| GLUTEN | Check the broth label |
| NUT | Check labels |

# Chorizo chicken

Chorizo is a tasty, spicy, Spanish sausage that brings chicken and/or roasted vegetables to life. If you've never tried chorizo before, go for a mild one first.

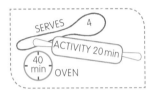

SERVES 4

ACTIVITY 20 min

40 min OVEN

## MAIN TASKS
- Brushing
- Chopping
- Handling raw meat
- Juicing
- Sprinkling

## VARIATIONS
Swap tomatoes for chunks of courgette or baby carrots. **(v)** Swap chicken for courgette, aubergine and red pepper cut into chunks and leave out the chorizo.

## ALLERGY INFO

| | |
|---|---|
| DAIRY | No dairy |
| EGG | No egg |
| GLUTEN | No gluten |
| NUT | Check labels |

## What you need
- 2 tbsp olive oil
- 6 skin-on chicken thighs
- 400g baby potatoes
- 6 cloves of garlic
- 120g chorizo
- 6 cherry tomatoes
- ½ an orange
- ⅛ tsp salt
- 1 tbsp dried mixed herbs

## Adult prep
- Preheat oven to 190°C/375°F/Gas 5.
- Lay out: ingredients, roasting tin, pastry brush, chopping board, child-safe or table knife, juicer, mixing spoon and small jug.

**TOP TIP!**

Try to space all the ingredients out in the tin and tuck the chorizo chunks underneath the chicken to stop them burning.

## How to make

**1** Put 1 tbsp of the olive oil into the roasting tin and spread it all around the bottom with a pastry brush.

**2** Put the chicken in the tin. Wash your hands after touching raw meat.

**3** Put the potatoes and garlic cloves (no need to peel) in the tin.

**4** Chop the chorizo into large chunks and put them into the tin.

**5** Chop the tomatoes in half and put them into the tin.

**6** Squeeze the juice from the orange into a small jug.

**7** Put 1 tbsp olive oil in the jug and mix it into the orange juice.

**8** Pour the juice and oil mix all over the chicken.

**9** Sprinkle the salt and herbs over the chicken.

Ask an adult to put the dish into the oven for 40 to 45 minutes until the chicken is cooked through. Test whether the chicken is cooked by cutting one thigh open. Serve with bread to dip into the orangey chorizo juices.

# Mediterranean kebabs

These colourful kebabs are a yummy vegetarian option for a BBQ or baked in the oven at any time. Delicious with warm pittas or served with the minty lamb on page 88.

## What you need
- 1 pepper
- 1 courgette
- 120g halloumi cheese
- ½ a lemon
- 2 tsp dried mint
- 2 tbsp olive oil

## Adult prep
- Preheat oven to 200°C/390°F/Gas 6.
- Cut the pepper in half.
- Lay out: ingredients, mixing bowl, mixing spoon, table or child-safe knife, chopping board, juicer, 4 kebab sticks and baking tray or grill rack.

### TOP TIP!
If using wooden kebab sticks, soak them in water first for at least 10 minutes before using to help stop them burning.

## How to make

1 Pull the stalk off the pepper and throw it away. Wash the pepper in cold water to clean off the seeds.

2 Chop the stalk off the end of the courgette and throw it away.

3 Chop the pepper, courgette and halloumi into big chunks and put them into the bowl.

4 Squeeze the juice from the lemon into the bowl.

5 Add the dried mint and olive oil to the bowl and give it all a good mix.

6 Put a bit of courgette, then pepper, then halloumi onto the kebab sticks and then again another two times. Do this again with the other sticks until you have used up all the chunks. (Take a look at page 31 for the safest way to thread skewers.)

7 Put the kebabs on a baking tray or grill rack.

Ask an adult to put the kebabs in the oven for 15 to 20 minutes, or grill for 10 minutes, turning halfway through

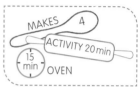

MAKES 4
ACTIVITY 20 min
15 min OVEN

## MAIN TASKS
- Chopping
- Juicing
- Mixing
- Threading on skewers

## ALLERGY INFO

| DAIRY | Swap halloumi for another vegetable |
|---|---|
| EGG | No egg |
| GLUTEN | No gluten |
| NUT | Check labels |

# Moroccan tagine

A tagine is the name of the clay pot that this yummy, sweet North African stew is traditionally cooked in. It can be made with any meat or just vegetables and in any oven-proof dish with a lid.

SERVES 4
ACTIVITY 20 min
90 min OVEN

## MAIN TASKS
• Chopping
• Handling raw meat
• Mixing

## VARIATIONS
Add other veg like peppers, aubergine or spinach. **(v)** Swap meat for tinned chickpeas, spinach and red pepper cut into chunks.

## ALLERGY INFO

| DAIRY | No dairy |
|-------|----------|
| EGG | No egg |
| GLUTEN | No gluten |
| NUT | Check labels |

**TOP TIP!**

Measure out a big batch of tagine spices in the jar, label it and use 1 tsp each time for Step 6.

## What you need
• 350g diced lamb
• 1 courgette
• 8 dried apricots
• 4 tbsp sultanas or raisins
• 1 tsp honey
• 1 x 400g tin of chopped tomatoes
• 2 garlic cloves
• ¼ tsp cinnamon
• ¼ tsp cumin
• ¼ tsp turmeric
• ⅛ tsp paprika

## Adult prep
• Preheat oven to 150°C/300°F/Gas 2.
• Open the tin of tomatoes.
• Lay out: ingredients, pan or oven dish with lid, table or child-safe knife, chopping board, mixing spoon and pot or jar with lid.

## How to make

**1** Put the diced lamb into the pan. Wash your hands after touching raw meat.

**2** Chop the stalk off the end of the courgette and throw it away. Chop the rest into little chunks and put them into the pan.

**3** Chop the apricots in half and put them into the pan.

**4** Put the sultanas, honey, chopped tomatoes and garlic cloves into the pan. Use a spoon to scrape out any tomatoes left in the tin – never put your hand inside a tin.

**5** Put the cinnamon, cumin, turmeric and paprika into a jar. Put a lid on and shake to mix them up.

**6** Tip the spices into the pan and give it all a good mix.

**7** Put the lid on.

Ask an adult to put the tagine into the oven for 1½ hours (or use a pressure or slow cooker) until the lamb is soft. Serve with couscous and cumin flatbreads (page 60).

# Super stew

If you're doing the 'eat-a-rainbow' challenge (page 120), this super stew will give you a point for every colour in one go.

## What you need

- 1 x 400g tin of haricot beans in water
- 1 x 400g tin of chopped tomatoes
- 8 pork sausages
- 8 baby sweetcorn cobs
- 4 shallots
- 2 handfuls of washed spinach leaves
- 150g baby carrots, washed
- 2 tsp dried herbs or fresh chopped herbs
- ⅛ tsp salt
- ⅛ tsp smoked paprika

## Adult prep

- Preheat oven to 150°C/300°F/Gas 2.
- Cut the root ends off the shallots.
- Open the tins.
- Lay out: ingredients, large oven-proof dish with lid, child-safe scissors and mixing spoon.

## How to make

1 Tip the haricot beans and chopped tomatoes into the dish. Use a spoon to scrape out any beans or tomatoes left inside the tin – never put your hand inside a tin.

2 Use child-safe scissors to snip each sausage into 3 chunks. Put the chunks into the dish. Wash your hands after touching raw meat.

3 Break the sweetcorn cobs in half and put them into the dish.

4 Peel the shallots and put them into the dish.

5 Put the spinach, carrots, herbs, salt and smoked paprika into the dish

6 Give it all a good mix.

Ask an adult to put the stew into the oven for 1½ hours or use a pressure or slow cooker. Serve with mashed potato or couscous.

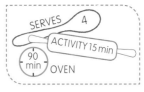

SERVES 4
ACTIVITY 15 min
90 min OVEN

## MAIN TASKS

- Handing raw meat
- Snipping
- Peeling
- Mixing

## VARIATIONS

Lots of vegetables work well in this stew so change the recipe depending on what you like the look of in the shops. **(v)** Leave out the sausages or use vegetarian ones.

## ALLERGY INFO

| | |
|---|---|
| DAIRY | No dairy |
| EGG | No egg |
| GLUTEN | No gluten |
| NUT | Check labels |

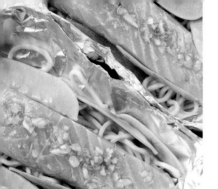

**BUDDING COOK**

# Teriyaki salmon noodles

Next time the family fancies a takeaway, try this easy, tasty noodle dish instead. You can even eat out of the foil parcels to save washing up!

SERVES 4
ACTIVITY 15 min
20 min OVEN

## MAIN TASKS
- Mixing
- Peeling
- Handling raw fish
- Brushing
- Wrapping

## VARIATIONS
Swap sugar snap peas for French beans. Swap the salmon for a different fish. **(v)** Swap salmon for tofu.

## ALLERGY INFO

| DAIRY | No dairy |
|---|---|
| EGG | Cook some egg-free dried noodles to use |
| GLUTEN | Avoid |
| NUT | Check labels |

## What you need
- 240g cooked egg noodles
- 1 tsp light soy sauce
- 1 garlic clove
- 1.5 cm bit of fresh ginger
- 1 tsp runny honey
- 2 tbsp teriyaki sauce
- 4 boneless salmon fillets
- 24 sugar snap peas or mangetout

### Adult prep
- Preheat oven to 180°C/350°F/Gas 4.
- Peel and finely chop the ginger.
- Lay out: ingredients, mixing bowl, mixing spoon, 4 sheets of foil big enough to wrap the fillets, rolling pin, garlic press, pastry brush and spatula.

## How to make

**1** Put the noodles and the soy sauce into the bowl and give them a good mix.

**2** Put a handful of noodles onto each sheet of foil.

**3** Bash the garlic with the rolling pin until the skin starts to come loose. Peel the garlic and then crush it through the garlic press.

**4** Put the crushed garlic, ginger, honey and teriyaki sauce into the bowl and mix them all together.

**5** Put each bit of salmon on top of each 'bed' of noodles.

**6** Brush the teriyaki mix all over each bit of salmon. Scrape any leftover mix onto the salmon.

**7** Put 6 sugar snap peas on top of each bit of salmon.

**8** Put the sides of the foil together and fold over the top and sides to wrap up the salmon in a parcel.

Ask an adult to **put the parcels in the oven for 20 minutes until the salmon is cooked through.**

# Veg-in-the-hole

It's not toad-in-the-hole, it's a vegetable version of this classic family meal. If you want to add meat, just pop in a few cooked cocktail sausages.

## What you need

- 1 tsp oil
- 65g (½ cup) plain flour
- 120ml (½ cup) milk
- ⅛ tsp salt
- 1 egg
- 6 sprigs of thyme
- 30g (⅓ cup) Cheddar cheese
- 60g broccoli
- 3 cherry tomatoes

## Adult prep

- Preheat oven to 200°C/390°F/Gas 6.
- Grate the cheese (an older child could do this).
- Lay out: ingredients, 18 cm metal pie dish or cake tin, pastry brush, mixing bowl, whisk, mixing spoon, table or child-safe knife and chopping board.

## How to make

1 Brush oil all over the bottom and sides of the metal dish.

2 Put the flour, milk and salt into the bowl.

3 Break the egg into the bowl.

4 Whisk up the mix until there are no lumps.

5 Pull the leaves off the thyme sprigs and put them into the bowl.

6 Put the grated cheese into the bowl and give it all a mix.

7 Pour the mix into the metal dish.

8 Tear the broccoli into little bits and put them, spaced out, in the dish.

9 Chop the tomatoes into quarters (4 bits) and put them, spaced out, in the dish.

Ask an adult to put the dish into the oven for 30 minutes.

SERVES 2
ACTIVITY 20 min
30 min OVEN

## MAIN TASKS

- Brushing
- Whisking
- Chopping
- Tearing

## VARIATIONS

Swap the broccoli or tomatoes for other veg like French beans, peppers or courgettes.

## ALLERGY INFO

| DAIRY | Use dairy-free milk and leave out the cheese |
| --- | --- |
| EGG | Avoid |
| GLUTEN | Use gluten-free flour |
| NUT | Check labels |

# Baked bean pasties

The filling for these is one of my youngest daugter's recipe inventions – a twist on jacket potato and beans!

MAKES 4
ACTIVITY 30 min
30 min
OVEN

## MAIN TASKS
- Using a microwave
- Dusting
- Rolling
- Chopping
- Mixing
- Wrapping
- Breaking eggs
- Brushing

## VARIATIONS
Swap potato for sweet potato and/or swap French beans for peas.

## ALLERGY INFO

| | |
|---|---|
| DAIRY | Use dairy-free pastry and leave out the cheese |
| EGG | Brush pasties with milk |
| GLUTEN | Use gluten-free pastry |
| NUT | Check labels |

## What you need
- 150g potatoes
- 450g shortcrust pastry (shop-bought or double the recipe on page 61)
- 1 tbsp flour for dusting
- 75g green beans
- 200g tin of baked beans
- 30g (⅓ cup) Cheddar cheese
- 1 egg

## Adult prep
- Preheat oven to 200°C/390°F/Gas 6.
- Grate the cheese (an older child could do this).
- Open the baked bean tin.
- Be ready to help use the microwave in Step 1.
- Lay out: ingredients, table or child-safe knife, mixing bowl, rolling pin, mixing spoon, baking tray, small bowl or mug, fork and pastry brush.

## How to make

**1** Put the potatoes into the microwave for 3 minutes so they are soft enough to chop easily.

**2** Cut the pastry into quarters (4 bits).

**3** Dust a bit of flour onto the worktop or table. Roll each bit of pastry out into 4 flat circles.

**4** Chop the potatoes and green beans into small chunks and put them in the mixing bowl.

**5** Put the baked beans and grated cheese into the mixing bowl. Use a spoon to scrape out any beans left in the tin – never put your hand inside.

**6** Give it all a good mix.

**7** Put two spoonfuls of the filling mix onto each pastry circle.

**8** Fold the circles in half. Fold the edges over and pinch so the mix is wrapped in a pastry parcel. Put them on the baking tray.

**9** Break the egg into the small bowl and whisk it with a fork, then paint it all over the pasties.

Ask an adult to put the pasties in the oven for 25 to 30 minutes until the pastry is golden and feels hollow when you tap it.

# Ratatouille

Ratatouille is so adaptable – serve as a side dish, eat with a hunk of bread, dollop on pasta, blend with cream and tinned tomatoes for soup or bake with chicken and tinned tomatoes for stew.

## What you need
- 2 cloves of garlic
- 4 shallots
- 1 red pepper
- 1 aubergine
- 1 large or 2 small courgettes
- 1 x 400g tin of chopped tomatoes
- 1 tbsp olive oil
- 10 basil leaves or 2 tsp dried mixed herbs
- ⅛ tsp salt
- ⅛ tsp ground pepper

## Parent prep
- Preheat oven to 190°C/375°F/Gas 5.
- Cut the root ends off the shallots and cut the shallots and pepper in half.
- Lay out: ingredients, rolling pin, table or child-safe knife, chopping board and oven-proof dish.

## How to make

1 Bash the garlic with a rolling pin until the skin starts to come off. Peel the skin off the garlic and put the peeled garlic into the dish.

2 Peel the shallots and put them into the dish.

3 Pull the stalk off the pepper and throw the stalk away. Wash the pepper in cold water to clean off the seeds.

4 Chop the stalks off the ends of the aubergine and courgette and throw the stalks away.

5 Chop the aubergine, courgette and pepper into bite-sized chunks. Put them into the dish.

6 Put the chopped tomatoes, salt and pepper into the dish.

7 Tear the basil leaves into bits and put them into the dish.

8 Add the salt and pepper and give it all a good mix.

Ask an adult to put the dish into the oven for 45 minutes and stir the mix every 15 minutes (or use a slow or pressure cooker).

SERVES 4
ACTIVITY 30 min
45 min OVEN

## MAIN TASKS
- Peeling
- Chopping
- Mixing

## ALLERGY INFO

| DAIRY | No dairy |
| --- | --- |
| EGG | No egg |
| GLUTEN | No gluten |
| NUT | Check labels |

**TOP TIP!**

Make a big batch of ratatouille, eat some straight away and keep the rest in the fridge or freezer ready to use in other things.

# Sweet endings

Everyone likes a sweet ending to round off a satisfying lunch or dinner. This selection of tasty crowd-pleasers should do the job!

 **EASY PEASY**

Baked cheesecake **102**

Cherry clafoutis **103**

Topsy-turvy tart **104**

Tremendous trifle **105**

 **BUDDING COOK**

Apple roll-ups **106**

Mud pies **107**

No-churn ice-cream **108**

Pancake cake **109**

Pink crumble **110**

Stripy mango chill **111**

**CONFIDENT CHEF**

Almond cake **112**

Fruity yoghurt **113**

# Baked cheesecake

Get the fantastic flavour of a cheesecake without having to wait for it to set in the fridge.

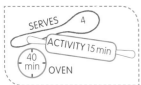

SERVES 4
ACTIVITY 15 min
40 min OVEN

## MAIN TASKS
- Breaking eggs
- Whisking
- Folding

## VARIATION
Swap berries for any fruit you like.

## ALLERGY INFO

| | |
|---|---|
| DAIRY | Use dairy-free soft cheese |
| EGG | Avoid |
| GLUTEN | Use gluten-free flour |
| NUT | Check labels |

## TOP TIP!
This pudding is delicious while still warm from the oven or chilled from the fridge.

## What you need
- 2 eggs
- 65g (½ cup) self-raising flour
- 180g (⅔ cup) cream cheese
- 1 tsp vanilla extract
- 2 tbsp vegetable oil
- 4 tbsp caster sugar
- 90g (⅔ cup) fresh or defrosted frozen berries

## Adult prep
- Preheat oven to 170°C/325°F/Gas 3.
- Lay out: ingredients, mixing bowl, hand whisk, mixing spoon, spatula and 15 cm cake tin.

## How to make

1 Break the eggs into the bowl.

2 Put the flour, cream cheese, vanilla extract, oil and sugar into the bowl.

3 Whisk it all up until the mix looks smooth.

4 Put the berries into the bowl and gently fold them into the mix.

5 Pour and scrape the mix into the cake tin.

Ask an adult to put the cheesecake into the oven for 40 minutes until it feels firm on top. Slice to serve with cream and berries.

# Cherry clafoutis

A clafoutis is a baked batter pudding from France, traditionally made with cherries.

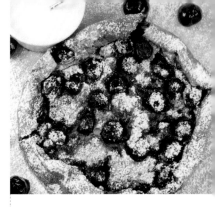

## What you need

- ½ tsp soft butter
- 140g (1 cup) frozen pitted cherries
- 3 eggs
- 3 tbsp caster sugar
- 1 tsp vanilla extract
- 4 tbsp plain flour
- 120ml (½ cup) milk
- 1 tbsp icing sugar (optional)

## Parent prep

- Preheat oven to 190°C/375°F/Gas 5.
- Lay out: ingredients, 18 cm metal cake tin or metal pie dish, mixing bowl, whisk and spatula.

## How to make

1 Rub the butter all over the bottom and sides of the cake tin.

2 Put the cherries in the cake tin. Spread them out.

3 Break the eggs into the bowl.

4 Put the sugar, vanilla extract and flour into the bowl.

5 Whisk it all up until there are no lumps.

6 Put the milk in the bowl and whisk again until the mix (batter) looks smooth.

7 Pour the mix on top of the cherries in the cake tin.

Ask an adult to put the clafoutis into the oven for 20 to 25 minutes until it feels firm on top.

8 If using, dust icing sugar over the top to decorate. Serve warm, with cream and extra cherries.

SERVES 4
ACTIVITY 15 min
25 min OVEN

## MAIN TASKS

- Breaking eggs
- Whisking

## VARIATION

Swap cherries for any fruit you like, particularly berries.

## ALLERGY INFO

| DAIRY | Use dairy-free spread and milk |
| --- | --- |
| EGG | Avoid |
| GLUTEN | Use gluten-free flour |
| NUT | Check labels |

**TOP TIP!**
Space the cherries out in the tin so it looks good when baked and every slice when served has roughly the same amount.

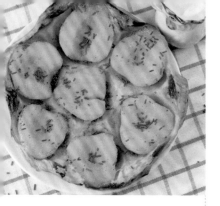

# Topsy-turvy tart

You make this tart one way, and serve it the other way by flipping it at the end. It's an easy way to make an impressive fruit tart with no soggy bottom.

SERVES 4
ACTIVITY 15 min
20 min
OVEN

## MAIN TASKS
• Dusting
• Rolling
• Sprinkling

## VARIATIONS
Use peeled, cored and halved fresh pears, or a different fruit like peaches or plums.

## ALLERGY INFO

| | |
|---|---|
| DAIRY | Use dairy-free pastry and check dark chocolate label or leave out chocolate |
| EGG | Check the pastry label |
| GLUTEN | Use gluten-free pastry and flour |
| NUT | Check labels |

## What you need
• 1 x 400g tin of pear halves (225g drained weight)
• a pinch of ground cinnamon (optional)
• 125g puff pastry
• 1 tsp flour for dusting
• 1 tsp chocolate sprinkles or grated dark chocolate

## Adult prep
• Preheat oven to 200°C/390°F/Gas 6.
• Open the pear tin and empty the contents into a bowl.
• Lay out: ingredients, 18 cm pie dish, cake tin or flan dish, rolling pin and plate.

### TOP TIP!
Have a go at making your own pastry. Puff pastry is tricky, but rough puff pastry is easy and works great in tarts (recipe on page 80).

## How to make

**1** Put the pear halves in the dish with the flat side down.

**2** If using, sprinkle the cinnamon over the pears.

**3** Dust a little flour onto the worktop or table to stop the pastry sticking.

**4** Roll the pastry out into a rough circle about the same size as the dish.

**5** Lay the pastry on the pears and tuck the edges around the pears like you're tucking them up for bed.

Ask an adult to put the tart into the oven for 20 minutes. Leave until cool enough to touch.

**6** Put a plate upside-down on the tin and then turn it the right way up. The tart should end up on the plate pear side up.

**7** Decorate the top with chocolate sprinkles or grated dark chocolate.

# Tremendous trifle

Layers of sponge, fruit and custard topped with whipped cream and sprinkles make trifle a dessert that is popular with everyone.

## What you need
- 1 banana, peeled
- 2 tbsp Greek-style yoghurt
- 1 x 400g tin of strawberries
- 8 sponge finger biscuits
- 120ml (½ cup) ready-made custard
- 120ml (½ cup) whipping or double cream
- Fresh strawberries, sweets or sprinkles to decorate

## Adult prep
- Open the tin of strawberries and tip the contents into a bowl, including the juice.
- Lay out: ingredients, mixing bowl, masher or fork, mixing spoon, flat-bottomed serving bowl spatula and whisk.

### TOP TIP!
If you're cooking for a big crowd, make the recipe twice in one serving bowl so you end up with one tremendous 8-layer trifle.

## How to make

**1** Put the banana and yoghurt into the bowl and mash with a fork or masher.

**2** Take the tinned strawberries out of their juice and put them into the mixing bowl. Mix it all up.

**3** Break the sponge fingers in half (2 bits) or into quarters (4 bits) and lay them in the bottom of the flat-bottomed serving bowl.

**4** Spoon and scrape the fruit mix on top of the sponge fingers.

**5** Pour 4 tbsp of juice from the tinned strawberries over the top.

**6** Pour the custard on top and spread it out to make a layer.

**7** Put the cream into the mixing bowl and whisk it until it thickens and holds its shape.

**8** Spoon and scrape the whisked cream on top of the custard.

**9** Put the trifle in the fridge for at least 2 hours.

**10** Decorate with fruit, sweets or sprinkles just before serving.

SERVES 4

ACTIVITY 20 min

2 hrs CHILL

## MAIN TASKS
- Mashing
- Spooning and scraping
- Whisking
- Decorating

## VARIATION
Swap banana or strawberries for any fruit combination you like. Tinned or leftover fruit salad works well.

## ALLERGY INFO
| | |
|---|---|
| DAIRY | Use dairy-free custard and yoghurt, swap whipped cream for dairy-free plain yoghurt and check sponge finger label |
| EGG | Use egg-free custard and egg-free sponge cake instead of fingers |
| GLUTEN | Use gluten-free sponge cake instead of fingers |
| NUT | Check labels |

# Apple roll-ups

A simple, fun way to make mini apple pies – great for a lunchbox, dessert or even an after-school snack.

MAKES 16
ACTIVITY 15 min
20 min OVEN

## MAIN TASKS
- Dusting
- Rolling
- Brushing

## VARIATION
Swap the apples for pears.

## ALLERGY INFO

| | |
|---|---|
| DAIRY | Use dairy-free pastry and dairy-free milk |
| EGG | Check pastry label |
| GLUTEN | Use gluten-free pastry |
| NUT | Check labels |

### TOP TIP!
Best with fresh apples but you can take a shortcut and use tinned apple slices.

## What you need
- 1 tbsp flour
- 220g sweet shortcrust pastry (shop-bought or recipe from page 61)
- ½ tbsp plain flour for dusting
- 2 eating apples
- 1 tsp milk

## Adult prep
- Peel, core and slice the apples into eighths.
- Preheat oven to 200°C/390°F/Gas 6.
- Lay out: ingredients, rolling pin, table knife, baking tray, pastry brush.

## How to make

1 Dust the flour onto the worktop and rolling pin to stop the pastry sticking.

2 Put the pastry onto the floured worktop and roll it out flat.

3 Cut the pastry into 4 cm-wide strips.

4 Put one apple slice onto a strip and roll it until the pastry wraps around the slice once.

5 Cut off the rest of the pastry strip and use it to roll the next slice.

6 Keep going until you have made 16 roll-ups.

7 Put the apple roll-ups onto a baking tray.

8 Brush a little milk on the roll-ups.

Ask an adult to put the roll-ups into the oven for 20 minutes until the pastry is cooked through.

# Mud pies

In my house, these gooey chocolate cakes are also known as mud pies. They don't look big, but you don't need much – they are super-rich and super-yummy!

## What you need

- 100g dark chocolate
- 20g butter
- 2 tbsp Greek-style yoghurt
- ½ tsp vanilla extract
- 1 tbsp caster sugar (optional)
- 3 tbsp self-raising flour

## Adult prep

- Preheat oven to 190°C/375°F/Gas 5.
- Be ready to help them use the microwave in Step 2.
- Lay out: ingredients, microwave-safe mixing bowl, mixing spoon, 4 silicone cupcake cases and spatula.

## How to make

**1** Break the chocolate into little bits and put them into the bowl.

**2** Put the chocolate into the microwave for 1 minute on low or 30 per cent power. Mix and put back in the microwave for another minute on low power. Keep going until the chocolate has melted.

**3** Put the butter into the bowl and mix until it melts into the chocolate.

**4** Put the vanilla extract, sugar and flour into the bowl.

**5** Mix it all up until you can't see any flour.

**6** Spoon and scrape the mix into each cupcake case. Make sure each one has the same amount.

Ask an adult to put the mud pies into the oven for 8 minutes. Turn the cakes out onto plates and serve straight away with cream and fruit.

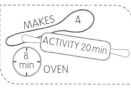

MAKES 4
ACTIVITY 20 min
8 min OVEN

## MAIN TASKS

- Using a microwave
- Mixing
- Spooning and scraping

## ALLERGY INFO

| | |
|---|---|
| DAIRY | Use dairy-free yoghurt and spread and check dark chocolate label |
| EGG | No egg |
| GLUTEN | Use gluten-free flour |
| NUT | Check labels |

## TOP TIP!

If you want to make these in advance, put them unbaked into the fridge or freezer. Then bake straight from the fridge for 10 minutes or from the freezer for 12 minutes.

# No-churn ice-cream

Easy ice-cream with no need for an ice-cream maker. Time to experiment with flavours!

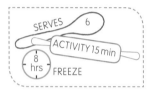

SERVES 6

ACTIVITY 15 min

8 hrs FREEZE

## MAIN TASKS
- Flavour selection
- Whisking

## VARIATION
Swap the orange for any flavour you like. Purée or juice the fruit you choose.

## ALLERGY INFO

| DAIRY | Avoid |
|-------|-------|
| EGG | No egg |
| GLUTEN | No gluten |
| NUT | Check labels |

## TOP TIP!
If you use a fruit with lots of seeds like raspberries, sieve your purée so you don't have hard bits in your ice-cream.

## What you need
- 240ml (1 cup) double cream
- 1 orange (or whatever fruit you've chosen)
- 160ml (⅔ cup) condensed milk
- 50g (¼ cup) dark chocolate chips (optional)

## Adult prep
- Cut the orange in half (or help purée whatever fruit children have chosen).
- Lay out: ingredients, 2 mixing bowls, whisk (preferably electric), juicer, mixing spoon or spatula and pot with lid.

## How to make

**1** Put the cream into the bowl and whisk until the cream looks thick and soft peaks form.

**2** Squeeze the juice from the orange and pour the juice into the other mixing bowl.

**3** Put the condensed milk into the bowl with the orange juice. Mix them together.

**4** Add the milk and orange mixture into the bowl with the cream.

**5** Whisk a little until everything is mixed together.

**6** If using, put the chocolate chips into the bowl and gently mix them in.

**7** Pour and scrape the mixture into the pot and put the lid on.

Ask an adult to put the ice-cream into the freezer for at least 8 hours.

# Pancake cake

This no-bake, layered cake is easy and fun to make and looks really impressive when you serve it.

## What you need
- 300ml (1 ⅓ cups) double cream
- 4 tbsp icing sugar
- 24 raspberries
- ½ a lemon
- 6 thin, shop-bought pancakes
- Extra ½ tbsp icing sugar for decorating

## Adult prep
Lay out: ingredients, mixing bowl, whisk (preferably electric), 2 plates, fork, mixing spoon or spatula, round dish, juicer, pastry brush and sieve

### TOP TIP!
Find a round dish that the pancakes fit into snugly so the cream doesn't ooze out the sides.

## How to make

**1** Put the cream and icing sugar into the bowl and whisk until the cream looks thick.

**2** Count out 12 raspberries and mash them on a plate with the fork.

**3** Put the mashed raspberries into the bowl and mix them gently (fold) into the cream.

**4** Put 1 pancake into the round dish.

**5** Squeeze the juice from the lemon and brush a little bit of lemon juice over the pancake.

**6** Spoon a big dollop of the whipped cream onto the pancake and spread it flat to cover the pancake.

**7** Put another pancake on top and do Steps 5 and 6 again. Keep going, finishing with a pancake on top.

**8** Put a plate on the top pancake to squash the cake.

**9** Put the cake into the fridge and leave for a minimum of 4 hours.

Ask an adult to help turn the cake upside-down and onto the plate.

**10** Dust the top with icing sugar and decorate with the rest of the raspberries. Slice to serve.

SERVES 6
ACTIVITY 20 min
4 hrs OVEN

## MAIN TASKS
- Whisking
- Mashing
- Folding
- Spooning and scraping
- Brushing
- Dusting

## VARIATION
Swap the raspberries and lemon for any fruit and juice combination you like.

## ALLERGY INFO

| DAIRY | Avoid |
|---|---|
| EGG | Avoid |
| GLUTEN | Avoid |
| NUT | Check labels |

# Pink crumble

If you think rhubarb tastes bitter, this crumble could change your mind – the strawberries take the tartness away.

SERVES 4
ACTIVITY 20 min
35 min OVEN

## MAIN TASKS
- Chopping
- 'Tickle fingers'
- Mixing

## VARIATION
Swap strawberries for 2 tsp sugar and 1/8 tsp ground ginger for a more traditional rhubarb crumble.

## ALLERGY INFO

| | |
|---|---|
| DAIRY | Use dairy-free spread |
| EGG | No egg |
| GLUTEN | Use gluten-free flour |
| NUT | Check labels |

## TOP TIP!
If strawberries or rhubarb are not in season, use frozen or tinned.

## What you need
- 200g (4 sticks) rhubarb
- 6 strawberries
- 1 tsp vanilla extract
- 55g butter
- 130g (1 cup) plain flour
- 2 tbsp caster sugar

## Adult prep
- Preheat oven to 200°C/390°F/Gas 6.
- Lay out: ingredients, oven-proof dish, table (or child-safe) knife, chopping board, mixing bowl and mixing spoon.

## How to make
1 Chop or break the rhubarb into chunks and put them into the dish.

2 Chop the green bits off the strawberries. Then chop them into quarters (4 bits).

3 Put the strawberry quarters and vanilla extract into the dish with the rhubarb.

4 Give it all a mix and spread it out flat.

5 Chop the butter into little bits and put them into the bowl.

6 Put the flour and sugar into the bowl.

7 Use fingertips to rub ('tickle') the butter into the flour until it looks like breadcrumbs (crumble).

8 Cover the rhubarb and strawberry evenly with the crumble topping.

Ask an adult to put the crumble into the oven for 30 to 35 minutes until it is light brown.

# Stripy mango chill

An instant chilled refreshing pudding that looks great and is perfect for a hot summer's day.

## What you need
- 240ml (1 cup) double or whipping cream
- 1 tbsp icing sugar
- 250g (2 cups) frozen mango
- 1 small lime
- 120ml (½ cup) water

## Adult prep
- Cut the lime in half.
- Lay out: ingredients, whisk (preferably electric), mixing bowl, food processor, spoon, spatula, juicer and 4 cups or glasses.

## How to make

1 Put the cream and icing sugar into the bowl and whisk until the cream looks thick and holds its shape.

2 Put the frozen mango into the food processor.

3 Squeeze the juice from the lime and pour the juice into the food processor.

4 Pour the water into the food processor.

5 Whizz up the mix until it is smooth. If it doesn't turn smooth, add a little more water.

6 Put a spoonful of the mango into each cup and spread it out to make a layer.

7 Put a spoonful of whipped cream on top of each and spread it out to make a layer.

8 Do Steps 6 and 7 again until you have no more mix left.

9 Eat straight away or keep in the fridge for no more than a few hours.

MAKES 4
ACTIVITY 15 min

## MAIN TASKS
- Whisking
- Juicing
- Using a food processor
- Spooning and scraping

## VARIATION
Swap mango for any frozen fruit or mix of fruits.

## ALLERGY INFO

| DAIRY | Swap cream for a layer of dairy-free plain yoghurt |
|---|---|
| EGG | No egg |
| GLUTEN | No gluten |
| NUT | Check labels |

**TOP TIP!**

For a shortcut, use squirty cream instead of whipping it up yourself.

# Almond cake

This is also called a Santiago cake, which is a Spanish cake made with almonds rather than flour and traditionally decorated with a cross. You can choose whatever shape you want to use.

SERVES 4
ACTIVITY 25 min
15 min OVEN

## MAIN TASKS
- Breaking eggs
- Whisking
- Folding
- Snipping
- Dusting

## VARIATION
Swap the orange for lemon.

## ALLERGY INFO

| DAIRY | No dairy |
|-------|----------|
| EGG | Avoid |
| GLUTEN | No gluten |
| NUT | Avoid |

## TOP TIP!
The key to this cake is whisking the eggs – the fluffier you get the eggs, the fluffier the cake

## What you need
- ¼ tsp oil
- 3 eggs
- 3 tbsp sugar
- 65g (⅔ cup) ground almonds
- 1 orange
- ⅛ tsp cinnamon
- 1 tbsp icing sugar

## Adult prep
- Preheat oven to 180°C/350°F/Gas 4.
- Remove the zest from the orange (an older child could do this).
- Lay out: ingredients, pastry brush, 18 cm cake tin or pie dish, mixing bowl, whisk, mixing spoon, spatula, sieve, paper or card, pencil and child-safe scissors.

## How to make

1 Brush the oil over the bottom and sides of the cake tin.

2 Break the eggs into the mixing bowl.

3 Put the sugar into the bowl.

4 Whisk the eggs and sugar until they look white and fluffy.

5 Put the ground almonds, orange zest and cinnamon into the bowl and mix it all in gently (fold).

6 Spoon and scrape the mix into the cake tin.

Ask an adult to put the cake into the oven for 15 minutes until it feels firm on top. While it is baking …

7 Draw a shape or a bubble letter onto the paper. Cut it out.

8 When the cake is cool, lay the paper shape onto the top of the cake.

9 Dust icing sugar all over the cake.

10 Carefully take off the paper to leave your chosen shape surrounded with sugar!

 **CONFIDENT CHEF**

# Fruity yoghurt

Transform plain yoghurt into all sorts of colours and flavours by making your own fruity yoghurt.

## What you need

- 150g frozen peach slices or strawberries
- 1 tsp caster sugar (optional)
- ½ tsp vanilla extract
- 250g (1 cup) Greek-style yoghurt

## Adult prep

- Be ready to help them use the microwave in step 2.
- Lay out: ingredients, microwave-safe bowl, mixing spoon, food processor, spatula, tub with lid and 4 teaspoons.

**TOP TIP!**

If you like yoghurt with 'bits,' mix in the cooked fruit without puréeing.

## How to make

1 Put the frozen fruit, sugar and vanilla extract into the microwave-safe bowl and give it all a mix.

2 Put the bowl into the microwave for 2 minutes. Leave it there for at least 1 minute to cool before taking it out.

3 Check whether the fruit is soft and breaking up. If it isn't, put the bowl back in the microwave for another minute.

4 Put the cooked fruit in the food processor and whizz until it looks smooth.

5 Spoon and scrape the yoghurt into the tub.

6 Put some of the fruit purée into the tub. Mix it into the yoghurt and taste a little on the end of a teaspoon. Keep adding purée and tasting until you've got the yoghurt tasting how you want it. Don't forget to use a clean teaspoon every time you taste test – do not double dip!

7 Put the lid on the tub and put in the fridge until ready to eat. Top with some fresh fruit if you like.

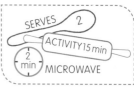

SERVES 2
ACTIVITY 15 min
2 min MICROWAVE

## MAIN TASKS

- Using a microwave
- Spooning and scraping
- Food processing

## VARIATION

Swap the peach for any fruit you like, but avoid ones with little seeds like raspberries or blackberries, otherwise you will need to sieve the seeds out of the purée.

## ALLERGY INFO

| DAIRY | Use dairy-free yogurt |
| --- | --- |
| EGG | No egg |
| GLUTEN | No gluten |
| NUT | Check labels |

# Useful bits and pieces

Here are some extra resources and easy-to-use charts that you might find useful for extra learning, to help choose recipes, or to make measuring easier.

# Measuring with cups and spoons

Anyone who uses American recipes will be familiar with measuring in cups and spoons (1 cup, ½ cup, ⅓ cup, ¼ cup; 1 tbsp, ½ tbsp, 1 tsp, ½ tsp).

There are some ingredients that are difficult to measure in cups and where scales are better, e.g. butter. But for dry and liquid ingredients, measuring in cups and spoons can be much easier (and quicker) for children. All they have to do is fill the right cup or spoon the right number of times. You can pick up these measuring cups and spoons in most kitchen shops. If you've never used this system, there are a few things to bear in mind:

1 Because you are measuring in volume not weight, conversion from grams is not precise, particularly if the ingredient if light, chunky or variable in size. Conversion charts, including the one on the right, are therefore just a guide.
2 To help ensure that children get as close as possible to the right measurement, it's important that they fill the cup or spoon to level. To learn this, get them to put too much in the cup or spoon and then level off the top with a hand or table knife.
3 Children can usually scoop up the ingredient with a spoon or one of the smaller cups, but for a 1 cup measurement, it it is easier if they put the cup on the worktop and fill it with another spoon.

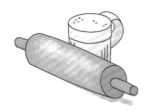

# CONVERSION CHART

## Liquids

| 1 cup | ½ cup | ⅓ cup | ¼ cup | 1 tbsp |
|-------|-------|-------|-------|--------|
| 240ml | 120ml | 80ml | 60ml | 15ml |

## Dry ingredients

| | 1 cup |
|--|-------|
| Flour | 125–140g |
| Oats | 100–110g |
| Caster sugar | 180–200g |
| Icing sugar | 125–135g |
| Ground almonds | 100g |

## Other

| | 1 cup |
|--|-------|
| Coarsely grated cheese | 90–100g |
| Finely grated cheese | 75–90g |
| Fresh breadcrumbs | 45–60g |
| Frozen fruit chunks or berries | 120–150g |
| Frozen peas | 130–150g |
| Sweetcorn | 150–180g |
| Chocolate chips | 180–200g |
| Rice (uncooked) | 185–200g |
| Diced pancetta | 130g |
| Cooked chicken chunks | 150g |

# Foodie activity ideas and resources

Here are some ideas of talking points, games and activities to help you engage your young chefs even more in food and cooking.

### Fruit and veg – get them talking!

Begin by explaining that a vegetable is just a part of a plant that you can eat. So weirdly, a fruit can also be called a vegetable. Different vegetables come from different parts of a plant – for example, carrots are the root of the carrot plant, broccoli is the flower of the broccoli plant, spinach and lettuce are the leaves, sweetcorn and peas are the seeds, green beans and mangetout are the seed pods and tomatoes, apples and peppers are the fruits of plants. Do children know which part of the plant the vegetable they're cooking with is from?

Have a chat about where fruit and veg come from – are they grown locally or abroad? Fruit and vegetables need certain weather to grow properly. The tropical ones like bananas, pineapples, mangoes and cocoa beans must travel a long way to get to our shops because they need very hot and humid weather. Certain vegetables like cucumbers, peppers, aubergine and tomatoes also need lots of sun, These grow well in our cooler climates, but only in the summer. In fact, most fruits and vegetables that do grow in cooler climates can only grow or be stored at certain times of the year. When they can't grow, you can still buy ones that have been frozen, tinned or that come from another part of the world. Discuss how the ingredient got to the shop. Talk about how it can be better and tastier to eat fruit and veg in season.

## Foodie activities – get them doing!

Having fun with food is great for fostering familiarity and enthusiasm for ingredients. Try these activities with children to get them hands-on with all different kinds of food.

**GROW THEIR OWN** Getting mucky planting seeds and then watching something go from seed to plant to plate is great thing to do with children. The best options are plants that germinate quickly like lettuce, chives, watercress and basil. You can grow these indoors all year round.

**PICK THEIR OWN** It's fun and inspiring for children to see fruit and veg growing and then cook with them. Sadly, most of us don't have time or space for an extensive veg patch, but for a similar experience, spend an hour or so at your nearest 'pick your own' farm.

**SHOPPING LIST GAME** Once they've chosen a recipe to cook, get children to write their own shopping list of what they need. Then let them help you find everything in the shop and complete the list. If they're too young to write, do some word recognition by writing out the list with tick boxes. When they've found an item, get them to find the word and tick it off.

**STILL-LIFE** Children are naturally programmed to be suspicious of food that is unfamiliar, which is why cooking with a certain food can be a good way to get them familiar with something and more likely to give it a try. Another fun way to do this is to get them to draw or paint fruit or vegetables in their natural state.

**PLAY SHOPS** Literally let the children play with food! Rather than plastic ingredients, let them play pretend shops or cafés with a few real ingredients. If you pick things that are going to be peeled or cooked, such as carrots or onions, you can usually still use whatever they've been playing with. If you don't want mess, just avoid things like broccoli or soft fruit that break up or squash easily.

EVE'S SOOTHIE RESAPE!

All, tropical frut exspe for banana.

— banana

— Mango

pipella

TROPIAL

**PLAY CAFÉS** Get children to set up a 'café' and serve you and the rest of the family. They can name the café, make signs and menus and take orders. They could pretend to cook and serve the food or perhaps even make some for real. It's usually interesting to see what they chose to put on their menu.

**THROW A DINNER PARTY** One way to turn cooking into something to keep children entertained all day is to get them to put on a dinner party. They choose what they're going to make, design and make decorations for the table, write out a menu and of course do the cooking. Do it for friends, just for the family, or to treat the grandparents. The food might not be quite five star, but there's something special about them seeing loved ones enjoying their creations.

**VEG CHALLENGE** Go to a supermarket or greengrocer and get children to select any fruit or veg, preferably something they don't recognise. You or they then have to cook something with it.

**WRITE YOUR OWN** Once they've done a fair bit of cooking, it's great fun to get children to write their own recipe completely from scratch. If you're feeling brave, you could then let them make it. It might not end up edible, but they'll have a lot of fun doing it and learn a lot. You will get some weird combinations!

**BAKE-OFF** Make it a bake-off: pick a recipe and get children to make their own version and pretend to judge it. Don't forget to award them 'star baker'!

**EAT A RAINBOW!** Some nutritionists suggest trying to eat as wide a range of colours as possible to ensure a comprehensive mix of vitamins and nutrients. Whatever the science, the eat-a-rainbow challenge is a fun way to encourage children to eat more fruit and veg. Draw an outline of a rainbow, get them to colour it in appropriately and then to mark or put a sticker on the right-coloured rainbow arch every time they eat a fruit of veg of that colour. If they like carrots, for instance, the orange arch will be very full. The aim is to fill up the rainbow and, in the process, broaden tastes.

# Allergy chart

If you need to consider any of the common children's allergies (dairy, egg, gluten or nut), this chart shows which recipes you can do using a traffic-light system.

Green means 'go for it', yellow means 'okay with substitutions' (ideas given with each recipe) and red means 'avoid altogether'. However, even if it says a recipe is okay, check all labels for allergens as different producers may include different ingredients.

| RECIPES | Dairy | Egg | Gluten | Nut |
|---|---|---|---|---|
| Pink smoothie – page 44 | 🟡 | 🟢 | 🟢 | 🟢 |
| Tropical smoothie – page 45 | 🟢 | 🟢 | 🟢 | 🟢 |
| Pick 'n' mix granola – page 46 | 🟢 | 🟢 | 🟡 | 🟡 |
| Egg mug – page 48 | 🟡 | 🔴 | 🟢 | 🟢 |
| Tray-bake pancakes – page 49 | 🟡 | 🔴 | 🟡 | 🟢 |
| Basic bread rolls – page 50 | 🟢 | 🟢 | 🔴 | 🟢 |
| Hot choc porridge – page 51 | 🟡 | 🟢 | 🟡 | 🟢 |
| Cauliflower bhajis – page 54 | 🟢 | 🟢 | 🟡 | 🟢 |
| Easy eggs Florentine – page 55 | 🟡 | 🟡 | 🟢 | 🟢 |
| Pea green soup – page 56 | 🟡 | 🟢 | 🟢 | 🟡 |
| Potato patties – page 57 | 🟡 | 🟡 | 🟡 | 🟢 |

| RECIPES | Dairy | Egg | Gluten | Nut |
|---|---|---|---|---|
| Veggie muffins – page 58 | ○ | ● | ○ | ○ |
| Baba ganoush – page 59 | ○ | ○ | ○ | ○ |
| Flatbreads – page 60 | ○ | ○ | ● | ○ |
| Shortcrust pastry dough – page 61 | ○ | ○ | ● | ○ |
| Mini quiches – page 62 | ○ | ● | ○ | ○ |
| Pesto – page 64 | ○ | ○ | ○ | ○ |
| Red pepper hummus – page 65 | ○ | ○ | ○ | ● |
| Quesadillas – page 66 | ○ | ○ | ○ | ○ |
| Roots soup – page 67 | ○ | ○ | ○ | ○ |
| American-style cookies – page 70 | ○ | ○ | ○ | ○ |
| Chocolate chip mince pies – page 71 | ○ | ○ | ○ | ○ |
| Fairy cakes 5 ways – page 72 | ○ | ○ | ○ | ○ |
| Tricolore sticks – page 75 | ○ | ○ | ○ | ○ |
| Aberffraw biscuits – page 76 | ○ | ○ | ○ | ○ |
| Fruit pops – page 77 | ○ | ○ | ○ | ○ |
| Sweet biscuits 5 ways – page 78 | ○ | ○ | ○ | ○ |
| Rough puff straws – page 80 | ○ | ○ | ○ | ○ |
| Soda bread farls – page 81 | ○ | ○ | ○ | ○ |
| Cheeseburgers– page 84 | ○ | ○ | ○ | ○ |
| Chunky chowder – page 85 | ○ | ○ | ○ | ○ |
| Creamy veg pasta bake – page 86 | ○ | ○ | ○ | ○ |
| Crunchy pesto fish – page 87 | ○ | ○ | ○ | ○ |
| Minty lamb pittas – page 88 | ○ | ○ | ○ | ○ |

| RECIPES | Dairy | Egg | Gluten | Nut |
|---|:---:|:---:|:---:|:---:|
| One-pot Bolognese rice – page 89 | ○ | ○ | ○ | ○ |
| Chickadee frickadee – page 90 | ○ | ○ | ○ | ○ |
| Chocolate chilli – page 91 | ○ | ○ | ○ | ○ |
| Chorizo chicken – page 92 | ○ | ○ | ○ | ○ |
| Mediterranean kebabs – page 93 | ○ | ○ | ○ | ○ |
| Moroccan tagine – page 94 | ○ | ○ | ○ | ○ |
| Super stew – page 95 | ○ | ○ | ○ | ○ |
| Teriyaki salmon noodles – page 96 | ○ | ○ | ● | ○ |
| Veg-in-the-hole – page 97 | ○ | ● | ○ | ○ |
| Baked bean pasties – page 98 | ○ | ○ | ○ | ○ |
| Ratatouille – page 99 | ○ | ○ | ○ | ○ |
| Baked cheesecake – page 102 | ○ | ● | ○ | ○ |
| Cherry clafoutis – page 103 | ○ | ● | ○ | ○ |
| Topsy-turvy tart – page 104 | ○ | ○ | ○ | ○ |
| Tremendous trifle – page 105 | ○ | ○ | ○ | ○ |
| Apple roll-ups – page 106 | ○ | ○ | ○ | ○ |
| Mud pies – page 107 | ○ | ○ | ○ | ○ |
| No-churn ice-cream – page 108 | ● | ○ | ○ | ○ |
| Pancake cake– page 109 | ● | ● | ● | ○ |
| Pink crumble – page 110 | ○ | ○ | ○ | ○ |
| Stripy mango chill – page 111 | ○ | ○ | ○ | ○ |
| Almond cake – page 112 | ○ | ● | ○ | ● |
| Fruity yoghurt – page 113 | ○ | ○ | ○ | ○ |

# Index

# Acknowledgements

Thank you,
Sam Jackson from PRH for asking me to write this book, Leah Feltham from PRH, Peggy Sadler who brought it to life, Susan McKeever the editor and to my agent Heather Holden-Brown and all at HHB.

All those friends who encouraged me to write this book and motivated me when I needed it, and in particular Jo Spry, Sam Wilkinson and Emma Ince Goulding.

My after-school cooking group who were the guinea pigs for many of these recipes and whose enthusiasm was infectious and inspiring.

The fabulous group of grown-ups and their children who put the recipes through their paces: Bex Carter, Clare Catto, Karen Fewson, Kate Hillson, Kat Gilbert, Charly McNelis, Julie Morgan Webber, Sofia Paterson, Ros Phillips, Charlie Slight, Emily Whitechurch, Karen Wood, Anne Woolmer, Sarah Paterson and Jo Spry.

All those who organised and contributed photographs: Caroline Freebairn, Alex Ginn, Charlie Slight, Simon Gilbert, Kat Gilbert, Jo Spry, Clare Catto, Kate Hillson, Bex Carter and Kate Cole.

The *Tickle Fingers* social media community and all those who have taken the time to review, comment, or contact us. Seeing and hearing about people having fun or benefitting from Tickle Fingers makes all the hard work worth it.

My family for their love, encouragement and support, in particular my wonderful parents.

My rock of a husband for always believing in me and doing the illustrations.

And last but definitely not least, the two reasons I wrote this book. Thank you for your patience, trust and inspirational enthusiasm for cooking and life. This book is for you with all my love. Take it, use it, then make the recipes your own and continue on your cooking journey.